COMPUTER-ASSISTED RESEARCH:

a guide to tapping online information for journalists

By Nora Paul

The Poynter Institute for Media Studies

and

Bonus Books, Inc.

03   02   01   00   99   1   2   3   4   5

International Standard Book number: 1-56625-137-0

Library of Congress Catalog Card Number: 99-65936

Bonus Books, Inc.
160 East Illinois Street
Chicago, Illinois 60611
www.bonus-books.com

The Poynter Institute for Media Studies
801 Third Street South
St. Petersburg, Florida 33701
www.poynter.org

TABLE OF CONTENTS

Introduction to the Fourth Edition

They say that one Internet year, like dog years, equals seven regular years. If that's the case, the last edition of *Computer Assisted Research: A guide to tapping online information* is now 21 years old. It's way past time for an update.

In the 7 years since the first edition of the guide (1992) was published (in which the Internet was not even mentioned!), the Internet has changed almost everything about the way information and contacts necessary for reporting are found, processed, and managed. Government agencies refer reporters to their Web site for the latest copy of a report or study. Some companies no longer send out paper press releases, they are e-mailed or found on the Web. News libraries which used card catalogs to point journalists to the books they had available now create information-rich Internet pathfinders on their newsroom intranets. Reporters locate interview sources, both people and data, on the Internet. And those interview sources, once found, often prefer first contact by e-mail, not telephone. For good, or ill, the Internet has changed the process of news gathering more profoundly, in a shorter period of time, than any other development.

In fact, the Internet has subsumed the world of online information to the point that the guide should be called *Computer-Assisted Research: A reporter's guide to tapping the Internet*. Most online vendors of information have migrated to Web-accessible versions of their software and those who haven't yet will soon. We will discuss the impact of those changes in chapter 4: Types of Material Online: comparisons of commercial services and Web sites.

What hasn't changed is the mission of this guide. Originally conceived as a compilation of helpful handouts on various online resources, the goal continues to be to provide guidance in thinking about your news research and information-seeking tasks. I hope to help you develop your knowledge and use of the information goldmines, and to hone your ability to avoid the information slagheaps found on the Internet.

This is not the guide to go to for technical information or specifics about software – there are plenty of those around. It is a resource guide and handbook for practical application of Internet-accessible resources and techniques in reporting and news research.

I hope this guide helps trainers and teachers to help others as they start tapping into online resources by providing practical overviews of the various "tools", specific guidelines into their use and cautions about their misuse.

The concerns about validity and credibility of information on the Web calls for a deeper treatment of the issue of qualifying Web-based information, you'll see that in chapter 5: Issues with Online Research: evaluating information online.

Some of the new resources and techniques that are becoming staples in the journalist's larder, like alert services and downloads of databases from the Web to use in spreadsheet analysis, will be covered in this edition – they didn't appear in the last edition.

The chapter on bulletin board services found in the earlier editions has been retired since, for the most part, those BBSs with the best content for journalists have migrated their content to the Web.

You'll see another change in the publication, back to a regular bound book. The three-ring binder idea was idealistic (it assumed we would keep track of who had the book and would send updated pages as a revision was called for – it never happened.) Unlike the third edition of the guide which had a complete version available online, this edition will have just some of the content on the Web site, but it will be kept more up to date than we had with the last edition. I will maintain on the Poynter Web site (*http://www.poynter.org/research/newcar*) a list of the links used in this guide. This should make linking to sites a bit easier, and provide updates as things change.

And change they do. I finished the chapter on newsgroups, with details about how to use DejaNews, about a week before DejaNews changed it's name to Deja and completely re-designed it's site. MiningCo., another site I referred to frequently, changed its name to About.com about a week before deadline! It's almost folly to write a book about an environment that is constantly changing.

In keeping with its mission as a training guide, I am adding a few sample questions or exercises to each chapter to make you dive a little deeper into the resources described because, ultimately, that is the only way to become comfortable in this medium – swim through it routinely.

Finally, the section on conceptualizing the world of the Web has been beefed up. I have found a high degree of miscomprehension about what the Internet is, and isn't. Some of the terms bandied around about the Internet badly need clarification. I hope to provide that for you here.

For the first few years of the Internet, it was called the "information superhighway." Many experienced it more as a bumpy and uncomfortable side road than a well-paved thoroughfare. Then the experience of using the Internet was referred to as "surfing," but, like surfing, it was an exhausting exercise in paddling out to where you think you need to be only to be thrown back to shore again. I like to think of using the Internet as pearl-diving, being targeted and focused on your goal and developing the skill to dive down to where you need to go. I hope this guide will help you develop your capacity to use the Internet and to get to those pearls that will help your reporting be complete, clear and compelling.

Although the framework for discussing the use of online resources is journalistic, I'm hopeful that the ideas of focusing on information tasks and applying the best tools is helpful to researchers and information seekers in all fields. As always, your comments, suggestions and complaints are helpful and appreciated.

A final note: Understand that the Internet is here to stay, but the sands are constantly shifting. New resources and techniques are constantly being developed, new software comes out that requires some time to understand. The Internet information space requires a commitment to constant learning. As philosopher Eric Hoffer said, "In a time of drastic change it is the learners who inherit the future. The learned usually find themselves equipped to live in a world that no longer exists."

So, keep learning and sharing what you've learned.

Enjoy,

Nora Paul
Poynter Institute
npaul@poynter.org
May 1999

ACKNOWLEDGMENTS

This may be the biggest section of the book. There are so many people who have inspired and supported my work in this area, a list of them all would be the size of the Manhattan phone book. Just to put it into categories:

Inspirational Internet trainers and teachers: To the hundreds of newsroom trainers and researchers, university professors, and consultants who are out there trying to help their colleagues and the new ranks of journalists learn how to use the Internet, thanks for the conversations we've had, the suggestions I've heard and the examples of approaches you've shared. In particular I'd like to thank in this category: Jane Briggs-Bunting, Sarah Cohen, Jennifer Lafleur, Steve Miller, Stephen Quinn, Randy Reddick, Robin Roland, Julian Sher, Jeff South, Roland Stanbridge, Peter Verweij, Mike Wendland, Margot Williams, and Debbie Wolfe.

The CARR-L and NewsLib Discussion List Communities: To the thousands of news researchers, journalists and educators who are members of these two discussion lists, I thank you for your sharing of resources found, and advice hard-earned. In particular I'd like to thank in this category Elliott Parker and Barbara Semonche, the owners of the lists, for their creation and maintenance of such helpful and generous communities.

The creators of helpful Web resources: So many people are creating wonderful material on the Web that makes the lives of researchers and journalists easier. In particular I'd like to thank Danny Sullivan for his work in tracking the hows and wherefores of search engines and Gary Price for his exhaustive lists of resources on the Web, and the Webmaster of and contributors to, past, present, and future, the Special Libraries Association, News Division Web site for the compilation of exceptionally useful resources.

Participants at seminars on Reporting with the Internet: Everyone of them has provided me with ideas and inspiration that keep my work fresh and my interest high. In particular I would like to thank Alex Gilev, a young Siberian journalist who attended a seminar and by the end of the second day had created a Web site for Russian journalists with the handouts from the seminar and a list of research resources.

The people who've given me a chance to hone my training skills and clarify my thinking: Thank you to the newsrooms in Minneapolis and Lincoln for having me come and teach in the newsroom. Thank you to NICAR, NetMedia, the European Journalism Centre, and the Institute for the Advancement of Journalism, for giving me the venues for speaking to and training journalists. In particular I'd like to thank Brant Houston and Milverton Wallace for giving me the chance to talk and making me keep my material fresh. And, of course, I'd like to thank the Poynter Institute, particularly Dean Karen Dunlap, my mentor Paul Pohlman and my friend and program assistant Cary Waulk, for letting me design and hold the courses I think our community needs. I do have the best job in journalism.

My colleagues in the Poynter library: Each of you helps with your suggestions, support and good humor. You are part of why I have the best job in journalism. Thanks Sandra Allen, Kathy Holmes, Sandy Johnakin, and David Shedden.

I would particularly like to thank Jane Briggs-Bunting, David Shedden, Debbie Wolfe, Pat Stith, and the CAR team at the *Naples Daily News* for reading the drafts and making suggestions, and Kitty Bennett, Bill Ruberry, Jennifer Small, and Debbie Wolfe for their extensive contributions to the text of the guide.

And, finally, I need to thank my dear boys, Nathan and Spencer Paul, for their constant support of their obsessive mother. Thank you, Nathan, for the shoulder rubs and pep talks. Thank you, Spencer, for making so many dinners and for telling me it's time to turn off the stupid computer and go take a walk.

The Four R's of CAJ

Computers have been changing the way journalists do their jobs ever since newspaper newsrooms threw out their typewriters and switched to cold-type production systems and television newsrooms went from tape splicing to digital editing. This change to computer-assisted production quickly and dramatically altered the way news is packaged.

The impact the computer has had on news-gathering has been more subtle, but no less dramatic.

"Computer-Assisted Journalism" is the umbrella term for the use of computers in news-gathering. This term can be daunting because so many different aspects of the journalist's job are lumped under it. Often, people hearing the term think immediately of expensive equipment, complicated programs and sophisticated analyses, used only in long-term, long-winded projects.

In fact, CAJ can be broken down into **four Rs: Reporting, Research, Reference,** and **Rendezvous**. Each of these four functions is critical to news-gathering. Each of them can be accomplished without a computer's assistance, but the use of a computer can speed up, simplify, and/or expand the range of the work. Here's a quick look at each of these functions, and how the computer assists:

Computer-Assisted Reporting

Traditional reporting techniques: gathering information through interviews, backgrounding, firsthand observation, working sources, getting tips, can be augmented by the use of computers. Computer-assisted reporting takes a combination of using spreadsheet programs to analyze large sets of records and perform calculations, statistical programs to analyze complex datasets, database software to build original collections of records and mapping software to display data visually in a geographic context. The information revealed from these techniques supplement the tried-and-true reporting methods without which you'd have numbers but no way to put them into context. The data that results from using these computer applications informs the reporting, spots trends, uncovers the hidden and provides independent verification of information.

Computer-Assisted Research

Research, like reporting, requires a special search or investigation. The distinction comes from the sources used by each. Generally, reporting relies on primary sources (firsthand, independent, original), such as interviews, observation or self-conducted computer analyses. Research uses secondary sources (made up of elements derived from something else) as the material being investigated. Together, reporting and research help form a complete news report. Databases consisting of secondary sources such as reports, articles, and studies can be used in computer-assisted research.

Computer-Assisted Reference

Reference is looking for those quick facts, spellings, definitions, statistics that add color or detail to the reporting. Reference works, such as dictionaries, encyclopedias, gazetteers, almanacs and glossaries, on the Web or on CD-ROMs provide handy and quick access to these small but essential details.

SOURCES

ARTICLES:

We're all nerds now, by Joel Simon and Carol Napolitano. Columbia Journalism Review, March/April 1999. *http://www.cjr.org/year/99/2/ nerds.asp*

ONLINE MATERIAL:

Bibliography on Computer Assisted Reporting. Compiled and maintained by David Shedden, Poynter Institute. *http://www.poynter.org/research/biblio /bib_car.htm* A very comprehensive listing of books and online resources on the use of CAR in journalism.

Handouts and articles on CAR. Poynter Institute: *http://www.poynter.org/research/car. htm*

IRE Resource Center. Investigative reporters and editors tipsheets and guides: *http://www.ire.org/ resourcecenter/*

BOOKS:

Computer-Assisted Reporting: a practical guide. 2nd edition. By Brant Houston, Bedford / St. Martin's, New York, 1999.

Computer-Assisted Reporting. 2nd edition. By Bruce Garrison, Lawrence Erlbaum Assoc., 1998.

The Online Journalist: Using the Internet and other electronic resources. 2nd edition. By Randy Reddick and Elliot King, HBJ College and School Division, 1997.

Power Journalism: Computer-Assisted Reporting. By Lisa C. Miller, Harcourt Brace Jovanovich College and School Division, 1997.

When Nerds and Words Collide. Edited by Nora Paul. Poynter Institute, St. Petersburg FL, 1999. (call 727-821-9494 for ordering information or visit *http://www.poynter.org*) A collection of essays about computer-assisted reporting by some of the pioneers in the field.

Wired Journalist: Newsroom guide to the Internet. 3rd edition. By Mike Wendland. Radio and Television News Directors Foundation, 1999.

Computer-Assisted Rendezvous

A "rendezvous" is defined as a place to which people customarily come in numbers. The "virtual communities" of the wired world are electronic rendezvous spots for journalists. The ability to hang out, listen in, seek advice and tap into other people's networks of sources is the newest and, perhaps, most exciting aspect of computer-assisted journalism. These areas include discussion lists, newsgroups, forums and chat.

Each of these four aspects of computer-assisted journalism requires different software, skills, and knowledge. Some are easier to learn than others. Some are more expensive than others. Some are more useful for certain types of reporting than others. Some you use at different stages of reporting than others. All are important parts of your work as a journalist.

If you are looking for more detail on the uses of computers for analyzing large datasets, crunching numbers with spreadsheets and creating original databases, there are some great books about Computer-Assisted Reporting. Those techniques won't be covered in this guide, although we will look at how to locate databases that can be downloaded into spreadsheets.

If you are looking for an overview of the other three Rs of CAJ, (Research, Reference, Rendezvous) this is the guide for you! Read on for information on the use of the computer to tap into databases, reference works, and to connect with people who can help you with researching and writing full, accurate, balanced and interesting news stories.

USES OF ONLINE INFORMATION: FOUR STAGES IN THE REPORTING PROCESS

This overview of the four stages of the reporting process outlines some of the computer-assisted research, reference, and rendezvous techniques that can help. The following chapter, "The Answer's Here, What's Your Question?", details specific information tasks and the resources that can help you get them done.

Story Idea

You need to find out what the "people in the know" know, spot trends *before* your competitors spot them. Otherwise, you'll just be following everyone else's leads. Here are some techniques for keeping up with your beat and spotting fresh leads.

- Join a discussion list related to your beat.
- Scan newsgroups on the topic you are covering.
- Monitor alternative sources of information on the Internet, check out e-zines and niche Web sites.
- Monitor relevant government agency or organization Web sites – check out their "What's New" or press releases.
- Set up a news filter on a topic you want to write about to get the latest news.

Begin Reporting

You need to get up to speed on the topic you will be reporting on, find out background information, do some reconnaissance on the coverage of that topic in other media, and locate people who can give you different perspectives. Try some of these resources to get information, locate sources and prepare for interviews.

- Check archives of newspaper and magazine articles in commercial database services or through individual news Web site archives.
- Find subject specific Web sites with articles or background material.
- Find "guide" sites that link to good resources in that area.
- Post requests to newsgroups looking for people with certain backgrounds or experiences.
- Locate government reports and statistics in gopher holes and World Wide Web pages.

During Reporting

You need to check the "facts" you get from interviewees, find and qualify the sources you need to interview, and follow up on angles uncovered during reporting. You need to think multimedia: your story will probably be published online; think of the multimedia elements that might help supplement the story you are reporting.

- Use ready reference sources to check spellings, facts, and statistics.
- Use people finders and public records to locate sources and background them.
- Use experts directories and locator services such as Profnet.
- Use government documents to check statistics given by sources.

SOURCES

BOOK:

Search Strategies in Mass Communication. 3rd edition. Jean Ward and Kathleen A. Hansen, Addison-Wesley Pub. Co., 1996. The classic on use of research for journalists.

- Qualify sources' expertise through checks of published material on commercial database services.
- Check out multimedia resources: photos, graphics, audio and video.

During Writing

You need to find "fun facts", quotes and story embellishments to brighten your writing, locate experts who can help interpret what you've found in reporting, and ensure you've kept up with the latest developments in the story you're covering.

- Find quotes and "fun facts" from ready reference sources.
- Use e-mail to correspond with experts.
- Create sidebars, information for graphics, and locate photos, graphics and art to illustrate the final package.

THE ANSWER'S HERE. WHAT'S YOUR QUESTION?: FRAMING YOUR RESEARCH STRATEGY

There are different stages in attacking a research task: defining the task and the question, selecting the right resource, and then conducting the research. This overview of these three stages provides a checklist for thinking through each step.

Defining the task and framing the question

Most people think the ability to do good research requires only good equipment, appropriate software, access to the services, and knowledge of how to use the resources. While those are certainly essential to conducting the research, they won't get you anything, but frustrated, if you don't go into the research knowing:

- what you are trying to do
- what you want to do it about

In other words, you need clarity about your information task, and about the topic.

In the past, when clip files were the only information resource available in newsrooms, the first approach to the information was by subject (or name or place). But now, with so many types of resources available, some better suited than others for certain kinds of tasks, thinking first about what task you are working on will help you narrow down the type of resource which might be most useful.

Once you are clear about the task you need to frame the question. What are the specifics you are looking for?

Use the task checklist to think through your information task and the "who, what, when, where, why, and how" question checklist to clarify and define the parameters of your question.

Selecting the resource

Which archive goes furthest back in time? Which directory is likely to have the kind of person you are looking for? Which service will be easiest and most reliable to use? Once you have defined your information task and topic these are the kinds of questions to ask in selecting which resource to use.

Use the "who, what, when, where, why, and how" questions checklist to think through your resource options.

Conducting the research

You know what you are trying to do. You're clear on what you are doing it about. You've selected where you are going to do it. Now, you have to run your research. There are some basic questions you should ask yourself as you start to do your researching on the resource you've selected. Use the research checklist to cover those "who, what, when, where, why, and how" questions you may have as you jump in and search.

Thinking through the "who, what, when, where, why, and how" at each critical stage in the research process will help you stay focused on your information needs, select the most appropriate and effective resource and develop an efficient and thorough search strategy. Use these guidelines for thinking through each step:

Framing your research strategy

- Defining the task
- Framing the question
- Selecting the resource
- Conducting the search

DEFINING THE TASK

Reporters and researchers have several specific types of information tasks they must do. Look over the following task inventory and think about these breakdowns as you define your own information task. Being specific about the task you must do will help you select the resource you would use to do it. After each type of specific information task are a few of the kinds of tools you might use to accomplish that task and the pages about that resource in this guide.

Locate people – primary sources

Reporters need people. They tell the stories and bring in the voice, experience and expertise that takes a news story from a recitation of what happened to a story with perspective, context and color. People give the unfiltered perspective and provide a variety of angles on a story. Here are some of the kinds of people-finding tasks journalists have and the resources that might help. Look in the sections on each of these types of resources for more detail about their use.

- A specific person you want to contact, you know their name:
  - telephone directories – 127
  - e-mail address finders – 29-30
  - public-records databases – 121-128
- People who might know a person who is in the news
  - neighbors directories in people finders – 121-128
  - news archive search on the person to get names of people who talk about them – 112-115
- An expert to interview on a topic you are covering
  - expert directories from universities, associations, think tanks, government staff directories – 153
  - the Profnet discussion list to locate university experts – 32
  - post a message to a discussion list on the topic asking for contacts – 31-39
  - check the newsgroups for people who sound smart on a topic – 39-46
- Someone with experience (has had that disease, experienced that event, has been involved in something you are writing about)
  - check newsgroups – 39-46
  - post a message to a discussion list – 31-39
  - check past articles in archives for leads – 112-115
  - contact an association – 70-72

Find documents – secondary sources

Documents give the background and facts about events, decisions, rulings. They are essential for getting specific details, for qualifying what people said, to see what has already been covered. There are a variety of types of documents journalists need, here's a checklist of some specific ones and how they might be found.

- Speeches from politicians
  - Governmental Web sites – 68-70
  - Personal Web sites of politicians – 79-81
  - Coverage from news stories – 77-79
- Press releases from companies, agencies
  - Company, agency Web sites – 72-73, 156
  - Press release databases – 155
- Court decisions
  - Law library collections – 156
  - Court Web sites – 156
  - (to get complete court records you must go to the source)
- Reports, studies, theses
  - Individual sites – 79-81
  - University sites – 73-74
  - Association sites – 70-72
  - Government agency sites – 68-70, 119
- News articles
  - Individual news Web site archives – 77-79
  - Commercial news archive collections – 112-115

Locate specific facts, statistics, ready-reference information

You need to fact-check, verify what someone told you, or find a fun-fact or quote to spice up the report. There are some great resources for quick answers to reference questions online.

- Find statistics on a topic
  - Government agency sites – 68-70
  - Association sites – 70-72
- Find quotes, sayings
  - Reference collections with quotations books online – 155-156
  - Specialized quotations collections – 155-156
- Look-up spellings, dates, specific facts
  - Ready reference collections online – 155-156
- Calculate/convert distances, measurements, currencies
  - Ready reference collections and online calculators – 155

Get up to speed on a topic

There is a great cartoon by Wiley Miller. A man is at the front of a line of people, holding a dart, his other hand over his eyes. He's standing in front of a huge bulletin board with words all over it: politics, economy, car repair, health care, television, aerospace, bioengineering, foreign affairs, country fairs, oil, vinegar, sports, stocks, bondage, oboe, septic tanks, explosives, liposuction, world peace. The Bulletin Board has a sign: "Today I am an Expert in . . ." The cartoon is titled: "How Reporters Start Their Day at Work."

This sums up well what most reporters and researchers deal with. You don't know what is going to be thrown at you when you get into work in the morning. Here are some of the backgrounding tasks you might have.

- Background on a country or place
  - Online gazetteers – 155-156
  - Government sites with profiles – 68-70
  - Tourism sites
- Background on a person
  - Reference collections and special biography resources – 155-156
  - News/magazine articles on the person – 112-115
  - Web sites by or about the person
- Background on a topic
  - FAQs (Frequently Asked Questions) from a newsgroup on the topic – 39-46
  - News articles – 112-115
  - Web site on the topic
- Background on a news story
  - Current news coverage and past articles – 112-115
  - Discussion on newsgroups – 39-46
- Find angles/slants on the topic
  - Discussion on newsgroups – 39-46
  - Find associations/groups interested in the topic – 70-72
  - Scan news coverage – 112-115

Staying up on your beat

Staying current and fresh on your beat, getting leads on stories and tracking trends before they hit the mainstream consciousness is one of the big information tasks of the journalist.

- Find out the latest news
  - Set up a news filter to catch articles – 53-58
  - Set up a message filter to find who is talking about what – 53-58
  - Check out E-zines or special publications on the Web
- Get story leads
  - Monitor newsgroups – 39-46
  - Join a discussion list – 31-39
- Create your contacts/sources list
  - Find leading experts through directories – 153
  - Monitor newsgroups – 39-46
  - Read discussion list messages – 31-39

Once you have defined the task you need to perform, think through this checklist of how to clarify the question you need to ask.

FRAMING THE QUESTION

This "who, what, when, where, why, and how" checklist will help you think through the details of your information quest. This merges some of the thinking of the Task Definition list with the kinds of specific things you should be clear about when framing your question.

Who

- **Who is the research about?** A politician, a businessperson, a scientist, a criminal? Knowing this will help you pinpoint the type of resource to use (a business, government directory, news stories, public records…)
- **Who is key to the topic you are researching?** Are there any recognized experts, spokespersons you should know about? Bring what you already know about a topic and who you know that knows about the topic to your question framing.
- **Who do you need to talk to?** Someone who has experienced something, someone who knows someone, someone who is an expert? This is part of task definition; knowing what type of person you need to locate can help you pinpoint the resource to use.
- **Who have you already talked to?** Who do they know who might help you? Remember to tap into the sources of the sources you've used – ask them who they would talk to if they had a question.
- **Who has done research on the topic?** Can you find someone you can contact who might give you some insight into the questions to be asking? Find other researchers/reporters/groups who have covered this topic and see what they asked.

What

- **What kind of information do you need?** Statistics, sources, background? Again, this is a task-clarification question to keep in mind as you frame your question.
- **What kind of story are you writing?** An in-depth analysis, a backgrounder, a first-day story, a follow-up? Keep clearly in mind the type of story you are writing, this will help you know how much and what type of information you need and help you select an appropriate tool. If you are on deadline, posting a question to a newsgroup or discussion list might not be wise – turnaround time can be too long. If you're writing a backgrounder, you'll want to get information from the most credible sources to get the most accurate picture. If you're doing an in-depth analysis, you'll want a variety of views from different perspectives. Each type of story will require a different type of research tactic.
- **What type of information will be useful?** Full-text articles or reports, specific facts, referrals to a person, public records? Visualize the kind of information that would really scratch your information itch.
- **What are you trying to do?** Confirm a fact you've been given, find someone to interview, get up to speed on a topic, background somebody, narrow a broad topic, fill in a hole in your reporting? Again, keep focused on the goal of the research.
- **What would be the best source of the information?** An association, a government agency, a research center, a company? Think about where you would go for information for your question in the "off-line" world and then focus on that type of source online. (Or, for that matter, get the information off-line – see "Before we start…" (pp. 17-19).
- **What information do you already have?** What do you already know about the topic or person? Don't forget what you've already gathered.

- **What would the ideal answer look like?** Would it be a great quote, a chart with statistics, an article titled "Everything you need to know about..." Envisioning the perfect answer will help you recognize it when you find it!

When

- **When did the event being researched take place?** This will help determine the source to use, which has resources dating far enough back. Remember that the world of Internet-accessible information is not very old; if you want things further back in time, the Internet or commercial archives may not be the place to go.
- **When did the event being researched end?** Is it ongoing?

Where

- **Where did the event you're researching take place?** The answer to this will obviously help you pinpoint local resources, agencies or news outlets to check into.
- **Where are you in your reporting?** Just starting (looking for background), in the middle (looking for verification of information), towards the end (looking to tie up loose ends)? This, along with knowing what type of story you are doing, will help you stay realistic about the kinds and amount of information you currently need.
- **Where have you already looked for information?** Keep track of places that have helped you in the past on this kind of research mission. Also, stay organized about where you have already looked, this will help when you bring in a researcher – let them know what you've already done, and what you found.
- **Where is the biggest or most relevant collection of the type of information you're looking for likely to be?** University research center, association files, specialty database, government agency? Narrow down the hunting ground by thinking through where the type of information you want would be compiled and maintained.
- **Where did the person you're backgrounding come from?** This, like knowing where the event took place, will help you focus on local resources and public records.
- **Where might there have been coverage of the event?** Newspapers, broadcasts, trade publications, court proceedings, discussions?

Why

- **Why do you need the research?** Reality-checking a source, looking for a source to talk to, reconnaissance on a broad topic, pinpointing a fact? Again, clarify your research mission.
- **Why must you have the research?** Can't pitch the story idea without it, can't prove the premise without corroboration? Keep focused on the goal.

How

- **How much information do you need?** A few good articles for background, everything in existence on the topic, just the specific fact? Answering this critical question will help you know when to stop researching and will keep you on task.

- **How are you going to use the information?** Anecdote to prove a point, illustrate a story statistically, quotes to provide voice? Knowing this will also help you know how to attribute and use the information in your story.
- **How far back do you need the information?** Most current year, back 10 years? Keep the range of time you are covering clear, you may select a different source and research technique if you are going back in time than if you just want the most current information.

SELECTING WHICH RESOURCE TO USE

This "who, what, when, where, why, and how" checklist will help you determine which information service, Web resource or research technique would best serve your need.

Who

- **Who might have the kind of information you're seeking?** Keep in mind your research task, (do you need an archive of news stories, a possible source of the latest statistics, credible background information?) and then think about who would provide it. You need to know what types of information are available from different types of resources (news archives, government agencies, public records services).
- **Who would have the most current/most retrospective data?** Some database services have more years available for the same publication than others. Some news Web sites have archives of articles, others don't. Some government agencies keep files of reports, some have only current releases. Answering this question might lead you to off-line research.

What

- **What kind of database should you use?** Are you looking for full-text articles, public records, statistics? Different types of information resources make different types of data available.
- **What services do you have available to you?** Obviously, this is critical to selecting your access options. This is particularly important when talking about commercial database services available through the Web or by direct dial.
- **What do each of the services offer?** Become familiar with the services' range of materials offered.

When

- **When are the services available?** You can't select an information service to use if it isn't available when you need it.
- **When should you use another service?** Checking in one resource first (the cheaper or easier one) but not getting anything might lead you to check with another service.

Where

- **Where are you most comfortable searching?** Which service are you most familiar with and knowledgeable about? This is particularly relevant when talking about Web search services – which of the search sites are you most savvy about so your searching can be efficient and effective?

- **Where do you have the best deal?** Database services offer different pricing options. In some cases, the commercial service might cost more than a Web alternative but consider the other aspects, search options, range of material available, ease of use.
- **Where can you get the best search support?** If your commercial service has a help line and you can get advice on the best search, it may be a better option to use than the cheaper route which makes you muddle through.

Why

- **Why might you use one service option over another?** Carefully weigh cost, range of material, ease of use when selecting the service to use.

How

- **How can you make logical selections for which resource to use?** The only answer is to consult an expert (your news researchers) or to develop a wide-ranging knowledge about your access options.

CONDUCTING THE SEARCH

This "who, what, when, where, why, how" checklist will help you to put your search strategy together and conduct the search. This is a general checklist. Look at the section on using Web search sites (89-102) for specifics.

Who

- **Who can help if you get into trouble during the search?** Be sure to have the help desk numbers handy for commercial services or know where to find the "help" file on a Web site you are using.
- **Who is the expert on searching in your newsroom?** Be familiar with your newsroom's research staff and their expertise.
- **Who can help you put a search strategy together?** You might want to do some research about your research and ask the advice of others who have covered similar types of stories. Again, tap into the research expertise of newsroom researchers.
- **Who are you searching for?** Do you have the correct spelling of their name, and have you taken care to cover possible nicknames or variations? What do you know about them to ensure you have the right person in the search results?

What

- **What kind of search will it be?** Is the database you are searching a free-text search that looks for words anywhere in an article? Is it a structured public records search where you must use specific types of terms and fields to retrieve information?

- **What search terms will I use?** Work up a list of terms that would be relevant to your search and be prepared to try searches in different combinations.
- **What will I do if I don't find any information (or too much)?** First thing, if you are using a commercial service that charges for the time you are online, GET OFFLINE! and regroup your search. In fact, this is good advice even if you are using a flat-rate or free service. You'll just waste time and get frustrated if you don't step back and re-think your strategy.
- **What are the search commands you need to use?** Make sure you are familiar with the search "engine" you are using. Understand the ways to state relationships between the search terms (and, or, not), understand how (or if) you can narrow the results. The first stop at any search site should be the help file and the next step in your research is to read it. Take time to learn how to operate the search engine so it can drive you to what you need.

When

- **When should you do the search?** Some services have cheaper access in off-hours or allow cheaper downloads after office hours.
- **When should you stop researching?** When your search results are totally unexpected – getting too much or too little material, or totally irrelevant material – you may need to re-group your search or take some time to learn how to use the search engine more effectively.
- **When should you stop researching – part 2?** When your question has been satisfactorily answered or you've found the amount of information you need or can currently deal with!

Where

- **Where should you do your search?** Within commercial services, know the range of the data in the variety of databases available, this will help in the selection of which database to use. On Web searches, choose the site that you are most comfortable with or the one that specializes in the type of topic you are covering.

Why

- **Why *are* you doing the search?** Keep in mind why you are searching, staying focused on the research goal.
- **Why are *you* doing the search?** If you are the researcher, should this search be done by the end-user? If you are the end-user, should a research expert help you with the research? (Much of this depends on the resource being used or the complexity of the research task).

How

- **How do you build a search strategy?** Be sure you understand how to link terms within the search (and, or, not).
- **How much is the search going to cost?** Know the cost structure of the service you are going to use, this can help you know when to abort a search. Also, think in terms of the cost of time – are you doing not just the most effective, but the most economical, searching?

- **How might you find it cheaper?** Be sensitive to the cost vs. return in your searching. If you just want a few background articles on a news topic that happened recently, find the news sites with free archives for the past few weeks before going online and paying for an article.
- **How will you attribute the information you locate in an online search?** Know the guidelines for attribution of sources depending on the type of resource used.

Before We Start: A Few Words About Online Research and the Internet

A few words about the Internet

- **It is essential**: A few years ago, the Internet was a "take-it-or-leave-it" type of resource. The range of materials was not vast, there were few tools to help you find things in it and it was hard to tell where the information came from. You could get the information you needed through "traditional" means. That is not true anymore. Many government agencies – national, state and local – no longer distribute information through those "traditional" means, it costs too much. If you want the press release, report, or latest statistics, you have to go to the Web.

  Often, if you want to get in contact with people, the best first access is through e-mail communication. Increasingly, the news is happening on the Web – the Web contains an important part of the story being covered (i.e., the Web site written by Eric Harris, one of the students who went on a shooting rampage through Columbine High School or the Web site of the Heaven's Gate cult which performed a mass suicide). Journalists without access to the Internet are, increasingly, shut out of important aspects of their news coverage.

- **It is a supplement**: While the above is all true, what is also true is the Internet is an important addition to the reporting repertoire but it is not a replacement of the tried and true techniques. Internet resources might give you a great kick start in your reporting, might help you locate that expert or track down that report you need, but it is just that, a kick start. You will still need to interview those experts and qualify the information in that report. The Internet might help you get a reference to a source but you'll still have to get it through regular channels.

  As with public records and court information, you might find a citation to the information you need but you'll need to do "traditional" paper-trail work to get the full story. So, as much of an advocate as I am for the use of Internet-accessible resources in reporting, I'm even more of an advocate of balance. The Internet is not the whole world of information necessary for reporters and it certainly is not a shortcut around good, thorough, traditional reporting techniques.

In this Guide, which sets out to explain the various tools of online research and pitch their use in reporting, there may be a degree of Internet boosterism. But, before we start, I want to say clearly that the Internet is an essential supplement to journalistic techniques, but it is by no means a replacement.

A few words about commercial services

This guide is different than the previous three editions because the world of online resources is different. The previous guides focused a lot of attention on the commercial services, many of which provided unique resources. But now the Internet and, more specifically, the World Wide Web has become the ubiquitous information delivery tool.

Most commercial database services, ones you would have dialed out to through a modem in the past, now have a Web version. Because of this, much of the reference in this guide will be to Internet/Web resources. The section on commercial database services (most now on the Web) will detail some of the changes that have happened in the marketplace of large data archives and the contents and uses of these types of services in reporting and research. But, because changes in these services are ongoing and the pricing options they offer are vast and convoluted, I will not go into as much detail about those aspects of the services. The directory of services in Chapter 4 will give you contact information where you can get user guides and the detailed instruction you need to use these specific services well.

A few words about how to approach Internet use

- **Think Small/Think Focus:** The cliché about the Internet is that it is the world's largest library but all the books are dumped in a huge pile in the middle of the room, and there is no catalog. Well, I agree with the image of the huge pile of material, but not the "no catalog" part. One of the problems with the Internet is there are too many catalogs. The search engines, directories and other catalogs of Web information are so huge in themselves that they are overwhelming. So, my advice is to think small about the Internet. Give yourself a break. Know that you can't know all the resources, so be kind to yourself. There are dozens of search sites, get to know two or three of them. There are thousands of government sites, decide the ones from which you have a consistent need for information and bookmark those.

    Analyze your daily reporting tasks, those things you have to do routinely and find a few resources that can help you do those tasks. If you are constantly having to find people then get to know some of the telephone/address services. If you routinely look for experts to interview, learn where the best directories are. If you cover a particular beat and always need articles and background on that topic, discover a few good Web sites with reliable content or directories to Web sites in that area. If just one type of information is the meat of your reporting (you're the legislative reporter and you need to constantly track legislative changes) then you might have a bookmark list with just one item on it – the state legislative Web site. And then let that be enough for now. Using a very small slice of the Web well is a whole lot better than trying to use it all and feeling frustrated.

- **Be conscious:** The main idea I preach to journalists using the Web is to be very conscious about what you are looking at and what is actually happening on the Web site you are using.

    If you aren't conscious, you can easily be misled by propaganda disguised as objective information (a medical Web site which is actually a pharmaceutical company's product). If you aren't conscious, you can be relying on outdated information that looks fresh (that great page about a country you are researching hasn't been updated since three governmental overthrows ago). If you aren't conscious, you can draw conclusions that simply aren't true (you don't find any recent examples of something in a database and conclude there haven't BEEN any recent examples – but the database hasn't been updated in 9 months).

In the section on using search sites, we will go into a great deal of consciousness-raising tips. In the section on Evaluating Information Online we will look at how to be conscious about the Web site you are looking at. Overall, the most important Web skill is how to be conscious when using these resources. It is essential to know how to know what these Web sites and services are, what they aren't, what they can do, what they can't, how they were created, who made them and why, and how to know if they are the best, most complete, most reliable route to the information you need. Consciousness happens with repeated exposure and, of course, an open mind.

- **There are no shortcuts:** The only way to get good at using the Internet is to spend time, lots of time, on it. As my professor friend Jane Briggs-Bunting says, "Surf early and often." Don't try and learn the ins and outs on deadline.

This guide, and the others cited on pages 158-159, will give you some clues, tips, and traps about using these resources in your research. But, just as with learning to drive a car, you have to go around the block a few times before you really know how to handle the equipment and navigate the territory. The exercises at the end of each Internet resource section should give you some practical experience with accessing and using these resources. Take the time to explore. Fall down the rabbit hole that is the wonderland of the Web.

A few words about what the Internet is, and isn't

What the Internet is

- **Amazing:** When you have fast access on great equipment to the whole range of Internetabilities there is no more dazzling an information utility. The size, scope, diversity and entertainment value of the information there is unprecedented. It really is amazing.
- **Uncontrolled:** There are no standards for the look, navigation, quality or organization of information on the Internet. That is part of the charm, and a large part of the frustration. The rule for Internet searching is, "Browser beware".
- **Easy to use:** After years of struggling with Unix commands and the frustrations of FTPing (file transfer protocols), the usability of the Web browser has made the Internet's information stores easy to get to and easy to navigate through. If you learn to open an address, click on a link, cycle back through retrieved pages, you've essentially got the skills required to use the World Wide Web.
- **Interactive:** E-mail "mailto" links, Internet relay chat, newsgroups – these are all examples of how the connections between computers on the Internet allow interaction between individuals and groups.
- **Multimedia:** In the "old days" of the Internet, files of different types (text, sound, images) sat as separate packages which had to be downloaded and viewed. Now, with the html (hypertext mark-up language) documents of the World Wide Web, these different file types are packaged together on a single page.
- **Inexpensive to use:** Careful shopping can get you monthly Internet access for less than the cost of a pizza and a six-pack. But the accent

is on "careful shopping". Look your options over very carefully. Most of the great sites on the Internet are (still) free access. If you really want to get online, have e-mail access, and be able to browse the resources of the Internetted world the cost of entry is not prohibitive compared to the large commercial database services.

- **3-D Information:** The text retrieved from commercial services, gopher and ftp is 2-dimensional, they have length and width. The Web, because of the hypertext mark-up language (html) used to create the pages found on it, is three dimensional. Web pages have length and width and they have the depth provided from hypertext linking to new pages. This 3-D information space provides powerful packages (but is also the source of some of the confusion of using the Web).

What the Internet isn't!

- **The repository of all knowledge:** If you ever want to drive a news researcher crazy, just tell them everything you need to know can be found on the Internet. While it is a vast "library of libraries", it is not the world's collected knowledge. If you think of available information as an ocean, the Internet would represent a vast atoll, increasingly well populated with information. But that other 80% of the ocean is commercial databases, CD-ROM products, public records and, yes – remember them?, books, which contain information and sources that are not, and may never be, found through the Internet's computer sites.

- **An information superhighway:** A superhighway conjures up a seamless ribbon of smooth asphalt, well marked and patrolled. The Internet is more a series of information relay stations. One computer link passes off your information request to another. Each substation has its own look, rules, and content.

- **Easily used:** Sure, it's easy to use, but its not necessarily easily used as an information resource. Knowing where and how to locate quality information, determining the actual source of the information and pinpointing specific facts can be difficult and frustrating. There are ways to ensure the resources become more easily used (develop research Web pages or well-organized bookmarks) but those are time-consuming to compile.

- **Cheap to get started:** Sure, it's inexpensive to use, but the cost of entry is not just the subscription. A 386 with a 14.4 band modem will not get you far on an Internet journey. You need to invest in a high-end computer (with at least 64 megs of RAM [Random Access Memory] and a 4 gigabyte hard drive) and a fast modem (at least 56k) or a direct connection to a high-speed transmission line.

- **Cheap to use:** Sure, access costs are low, but time is money! Staying focused in your research goal, having good guides for getting to where you need to go and stopping when you've found the answer you need will help keep the cost of your time online down.

Now, with this understanding, let's jump in the information ocean.

A Conceptual View of the Internet

The Internet has blasted onto the scene in most newsrooms.

According to 1998's Media in Cyberspace poll: *http://www.middleberg.com/sub_cyberspacestudy.html*, only 2% of the respondents said they did not have access to the Internet. That is good news.

The bad news, however, is that in many newsrooms access is from a single computer off in a corner. Even for many of those journalists with desktop access, the level of confidence in their use of the Internet is quite low, and their frustration level quite high. This valuable resource is vastly underused by many in the newsroom.

Aside from the lack of convenient access, part of the reason for this, I believe, is the lack of clarity about the component pieces of the Internet, how they can be used in reporting, how they can be used wisely and well, and how to avoid misusing them. Sure, everyone may be e-mailing, but are they taking advantage of discussion lists? They might be using the World Wide Web, but do they know about gopherholes?

In this section we will be talking about a conceptual view of the Internet, what the pieces of the Internet are, and how they fit together. In the following chapters we will look at the different component pieces and examine, in detail, how and why and how not to use them.

The Internet is called a "network of networks". Think of it like the telephone system. If you have an account with a telephone company you can tap into its network of telephone lines and make calls to anyone in the world who is also connected to the telephone lines. The Internet, this network of networks, can be tapped into if you get an account with a company that lets you access their connection between computer networks around the world.

This connection between computer networks might be through twisted wire cable, fiber-optic cable, satellite or any combination.

Like the telephone system, each station on this network of networks has a separate identification number, called an IP (Internet Protocol) address. This set of numbers identifies the specific computer network and allows computers to "call up" a specific computer on the network.

OK, folks, that's about as technical as I'm going to get with the Internet. If you want to read the whole history of its development and get into the nuts and bolts of its operation, there are some great guides (see the margins). My focus is what you can do because of this network of networks.

There is a suite of different information distribution and communication tools possible because of this networking. They can be roughly divided into tools that help you connect to people (primary sources, unfiltered information and conversation) and tools which help you connect to documents (secondary sources, filtered, edited information). Each of these tools require different software. They can be done independently (for example, someone might be able to do e-mail through their Internet connection because they have e-mail software running but cannot access the World Wide Web because they don't have browser software loaded.) This following listing gives an overview on the types of tools. Each will be detailed in the coming chapters.

SOURCES

ONLINE RESOURCES:

The Usually Useful Internet Guide for Journalists: *http://www.usus.org/* This site was put together by seven people from six different countries who had taken a Global Electronic Journalism course in Sweden. The guide provides a great overview in the journalistic context of different parts of the Internet and how best journalists can use them.

Understanding and using the Internet: *http://www.pbs.org/uti/* This resource provides links to many great online guides to the Internet. The links are well organized by categories (Internet facts and figures, Internet background, Internet guides).

BOOKS:

The Internet for Dummies, 6th edition. By John R. Levine, Carol Baroudi, Margaret Levine Young, IDG Books Worldwide, 1999.

How the Internet Works, 4th edition. By Preston Gralla, Mina Reimer, Stephen Adams, Que Education and Training, 1998.

People Tools: connection to primary sources – unfiltered comments, discussion, opinion

- E-mail (electronic mail): one-to-one message exchange
- Discussion lists (aka listservs): one-to-many message exchange – e-mail distribution lists
- Newsgroups (aka Usenet): publicly posted messages, like a bulletin board
- Forums: newsgroup-type areas found on Web sites
- Chat: "real-time" messaging, you see the message as it is posted

Document Tools: secondary sources – articles, reports, studies

- FTP (File Transfer Protocol): transferring a specific document (or file) from one computer to another
- Telnet: logging into a remote computer
- Gopher: an early index of the documents located in Internet networked computers
- Alert services: customizable filters which snag and send information items of interest – usually found as part of a Web site's service
- WWW (World Wide Web): the hypertext document space

For most people, when they say "the Internet" they mean the World Wide Web. In lots of ways, the Web has wrapped the various tools of the Internet into its information space. But it is important to understand the differences between these information and communication tools and to appreciate how they can serve various uses in your reporting and researching tasks.

So, without further ado, let's look at each of these Internet tools.

E-Mail

E-mail (electronic mail) is the common denominator of Internet access. If you have a way to get on and use the resources of the Internet, you have an e-mail address. And if you have an e-mail address, you have the means to connect with the millions of other Internet users around the world. E-mail allows you to subscribe to *discussion lists*, correspond with colleagues and contacts, conduct interviews and get leads to experts and sources.

E-mail in reporting and research

- E-mail allows you to send personal messages to individuals, providing more privacy in the correspondence. You might post a message publicly to a newsgroup, get some responses and then carry on the conversation through e-mail. Many reporters request that responses to a publicly posted message be sent only to their private e-mail address.
- E-mail can be a more efficient way to communicate with hard-to-reach individuals. Avoid phone tag or rambling voice mail messages by sending an e-mail request for information to someone. He/she can then answer, at length, at their convenience by posting a message back to you.
- Finding an e-mail might be the only means of reaching someone with an unlisted phone number.

- Through e-mail interviews you can contact people who might have difficulty communicating or hearing.
- E-mail can be sent after office hours, and there is a chance that the person you are trying to contact might check e-mail while away from the office.
- E-mailed responses put the answer into text form, making it easy (with their knowledge and permission) to incorporate someone's comments into your story.
- E-mail is the means through which you can subscribe to discussion lists.
- E-mail can be used to get alert services and notices sent directly to you.
- E-mail directories can help you find sources that you might not locate otherwise. Some provide profiles that individuals fill out about themselves and can be searched to find people with particular hobbies or who live or work in specific places. However, no definitive, all-encompassing e-mail directory exists.
- E-mail attachments of photos, documents and data can be a quick way of getting information from agencies and offices.

E-mail anecdotes

Stuart Watson, investigative reporter at WCNC-TV in Charlotte, NC: *The Dept. of Corrections and even local jails now send us mug shots as attached files. I was working on a story about school violence and the state Dept. of Public Instruction sent me school-by-school violence stats as an attached file – it was a small database. I could tell instantly which schools found the most guns, had the most assaults on teachers, or the most students suspended for drugs. Hear, hear for the attached file. No diskettes. No waiting for the mail. No traveling miles to haul around 70 pounds of gear to shoot a little 2" x 3" mug shot.*

Paula Felps, freelance writer in Dallas: *I was writing a piece on a man named Harvey Gerst who had opened a recording studio in Dallas. He mentioned he had written some songs with Roger McGuinn (of the Byrds fame). I looked in reference books and found nothing to support that claim. I searched the Web for a Byrds fan site, which directed me to an e-mail for McGuinn. We corresponded and he confirmed they had worked together and I got quotes from McGuinn on Harvey's work.*

Hurst Laviana, reporter at the *Wichita Eagle*: *On Aug. 18, 1998, an anthrax scare emptied the Finney State Office Building in Wichita. A day or so later, copies of a threatening letter left in the building arrived at a local television station and at the Nevada home of radio talk show host Art Bell. I called the Wichita station that carried Bell's show, and they referred me to Bell's home and studio in Nevada. The people there said Bell was unavailable and referred me to Bell's publicist in Oregon. I left a number with the publicist and figured I was at a dead end. But on the Internet I found a link to artbell@aol.com on Bell's Web site. I sent him an e-mail. About 90 minutes later the phone rang. It was Art Bell.*

An excerpt from the next day's story:

"McCormick said the first letter arrived at KWCH-TV, Channel 12, a day after the anthrax scare. A second letter arrived at the home of radio personality Art Bell, whose late-night talk show is carried on more than 300 stations,

SOURCES

ONLINE RESOURCES:

Beginner's Guide to Effective E-Mail
http://www.webfoot.com/advice/email. top.html
   Tips about using a good format, the right tone, and the proper use of greetings and signature files (your identification notice).

Everything E-Mail:
http://everythingemail.net
   With sections on e-mail directories, tips, glossary, software, books and resources, this truly covers the e-mail waterfront.

Trouble-shooting E-Mail Chart:
http://w3.one.net/~alward/etable. html
   Have you sent out e-mail and gotten back the cryptic message: Bad Host Name? This chart with help you figure out this and other e-mail error messages.

BOOKS

E-Mail for Dummies, edited by John R. Levine, IDG Books Worldwide, 1997.

Writing Effective E-Mail: Improving your electronic communication, by Nancy and Tom Flynn, Crisp Publications, 1998.

including KFH-1330 AM in Wichita. Both letters consisted of 11 pages and were mailed in Wichita on the day of the scare, the FBI said. Both copies of the letter are being examined by the FBI lab in Washington, D.C.

Bell said he had no idea why the letter was sent to him.

"And I'm not at all happy about it," he said in an interview from his home in Pahrump, Nev. "You might imagine it a hoax, but it didn't read like a hoax. It read like somebody who was aware of what he was doing.... There were specific demands and there were specific threats."

Not a major scoop, but it shows how e-mail can sometimes take you places a telephone can't. The publicist, by the way, never returned my call.

What you need to do e-mail

E-mailing requires e-mail software and the assignment of an e-mail address.

E-mail software: There are any number of e-mail software packages available. Some of the popular ones are Eudora, cc:mail, Exchange. The software is loaded on your computer or on the network your computer is hooked to and manages the various e-mail functions. In the past year or so there has been a proliferation of free e-mail services available on Web sites (see list at the end), so it is possible to have a company e-mail address, to use for official business, and a personal e-mail address through a Web site where you can do personal messaging.

E-mail functions: Whether you use a software package on your network or through a Web site, the functions of e-mail are basically the same. You receive messages into your in-box. You can display, reply to, forward, or delete messages. You can compose new messages or store messages in personal folders. Some software even allows for pretty sophisticated sorting so that messages coming from a particular discussion list, for example, are automatically sorted and put into a special folder. You can attach files (text, images, datasets) to e-mail messages. Attached files are the way many writers submit stories to publications. The software also maintains for you an address book of e-mail addresses you've used. Each of the functions work a little differently depending on the software package you are using.

The E-Mail Address: An e-mail address, like a postal address, directs the mail handlers passing e-mail messages through the network of computers to get the message to the right mail slot. An e-mail address consists of four parts. We'll break down my e-mail address,

npaul@poynter.org :

npaul	my user name : Poynter has a standard, as do many organizations, for the user name (first initial, last name). On non-corporate e-mail services you usually make up your own user name, however, some systems generate random user names, i.e., Compuserve's numbers. Some services have so many users you might have to chose a very unusual name because all the normal ones you would use are already in use.
@	"at", the universal separator between the user name and the rest of the address.
poynter	the host computer, the computer where my e-mail box is.
org	indicates the type of host computer (org for organization, gov for government, edu for university, com for commer-

cial, net for network – some may have two letters which indicate it is from a non-U.S. computer – see appendix for list of country codes.)

The "poynter.org" is also referred to as the "domain" – the Internet's name for a particular network or computer system. This name is a translation of the actual numerical IP (Internet Protocol) address which, like a telephone number, identifies a specific host on the Internet network. Poynter's actual IP address is 208.143.211.2 (IP addresses are always four sets of numbers, between 0 and 255, separated by periods.)

Since numbers are harder to remember than words, these IP numerical addresses are mapped to the domain name.

A software package called SMTP (Simple Mail Transfer Protocol) allows the transmission of messages sent between machines of dissimilar types.

Tips and traps when using e-mail

Verification

I imagine when those new-fangled telephones first started being used in newsrooms, the old-timers said, "How can you believe you're really talking to the person they say they are, you can't see them!" A similar healthy skepticism is being voiced about using e-mail as a way to contact and interview people. Ira Chinoy, while at the *Providence Journal* (he is now at the *Washington Post*), put together a few simple but important guidelines for reading and sending e-mail messages that will be used in stories:

Verify: Just because e-mail arrives with the name of a sender, there is always the possibility of a hoax. If you plan to quote an e-mail message, contact that person directly to confirm that they are, indeed, the author. (And if you can't, don't use it!)

Verify, part 2: If you got an anonymous call claiming something to be true, you'd check it out. The same rule applies on the Internet.

Verify, part 3: Some e-mail systems are capable of passing along, unwittingly, everything a person typed – even errors the sender thought she was deleting. This is not common, but keep an eye out for it. Check with the sender if you suspect a problem.

The rules of libel, slander and privacy are evolving in this new realm. Be alert.

Wise words from Ira, heed them well.

Also, keep in mind how easy it is for people to quickly create an e-mail identity. The use of free services and the ability to change user names has spawned the practice of "pranksters" who post messages under the name of someone who has just found themselves in the news spotlight. More than one news organization got fooled by the Timothy McVeigh messages in AOL after he was named as a suspect in the Oklahoma City bombing – "the mad bomber" listed under McVeigh's name was not him – as too many breathless reporters had claimed. Verify, verify, verify.

Netiquette

Netiquette, proper net etiquette, keeps the unruly world of the Internet a bit friendlier. Bill Ruberry, training and technology director at the *Richmond Times-Dispatch,* compiled this list of netiquette tips for use of e-mail:

- Treat the writing of electronic mail the same as writing a letter on company stationery.
- Check your e-mail box regularly and respond to messages within a reasonable time.
- Be careful with humor and avoid sarcasm. Electronic communications can be misunderstood because they lack the voice inflections, gestures and other body language of face-to-face conversations. A smiley face :-) (look sideways) does not always remedy bruised sensibilities.
- Do not send heated messages, or "flames." Let flaming be a one-way street.
- Don't use all capital letters on your messages. THIS IS INTERPRETED AS SHOUTING.
- Include a short signature file on your messages with your name, e-mail address, etc.
- Include brief, clear and meaningful titles on your messages so the receiver can have a hint about the contents.
- Never forward personal e-mail to mailing lists or Usenet (or to anyone else) without the author's permission.
- Copy some of the original message sent to you so your response will have a context. Use the > to indicate a bit of message which is being repeated (this is automatic in some e-mail software). But you don't have to send back the whole message which was sent to you.

Most important, remember that e-mail is not totally private and that anything you say on e-mail might end-up in the wrong hands, so always consider carefully what you've typed before you hit that "send" key.

Remember, too, that e-mail, like reporter's notes, is increasingly being used as evidence in lawsuits. Many companies are requiring that journalists delete their e-mail to avoid that possibility.

Check your company's e-mail policy to make sure you are using this tool on their time the way they have outlined its use. If your company does not have an e-mail policy, they need to consider one. Take a look at this sample policy from the Associated Press on Bill Dedman's Power Reporting site: *http://PowerReporting.com/rules.html/*

Spam

Spam messages, the junkmail of the Internet, are the bane of many e-mailers. These unsolicited messages should just be deleted, don't write them to say "Don't ever send me a message again!", all you are doing is confirming that someone is answering at that e-mail address. So, do what you do with that tire sale flyer or catalog of spiffy golf clothes – throw it out.

E-mail Hoaxes and Viruses

Nary a day goes by without some kind of message about a current e-mail-carried virus. At least once a week I get the latest e-mail hoax ("We here at Microsoft are testing a new service, send this message to 10 friends and Bill Gates will send you $1,000 just for being a part of it."). When you see these things that look too bad or too good to be true – be a reporter! Check it out. One of the best clearinghouses of various hoaxes and real and pretend viruses on the Internet is found in the Urban Legends and Folklore section of About.com: *http://urbanlegends.about.com*

Another good source for when these inevitably crop up is Computer Virus Myths: *http://www.kumite.com/myths/*

Finding E-mail addresses

There are a number of different e-mail directories on the Web. As we'll be discussing in the section on "people finding" you'll learn with e-mail directories that the best one to use is the one which has the person you are looking for in it! That might require some shopping around.

For researchers, the frustrating things about using these directories are not having a clear idea of where the information in the directory comes from, how often it is updated or just what the scope of the information is. There is such a variety of services, some with different special features, that the best approach is to keep a good list of services handy or use one of the sites which compiles a number of different services on one page and then just flip through them until, hopefully, you find what you need.

Basically, e-mail directories let you look up a person's name and sometimes designate a particular domain to look for it in. Some do only literal matches of the name, others might find "sounds-like" matches, too. The trouble is, with a common name, there may be a lot of "hits" found – you'll need some other clue to know if you found the right person.

General E-Mail Directories (primarily U.S. e-mail)

- WhoWhere: *http://www.whowhere.com.* Look for an e-mail address by just plugging in first and last name or go to advanced search and find e-mail of people who fit certain profiles in the "Communities" search (which includes city, state, schools attended, interests, groups they belong to, employers). WhoWhere found my current e-mail address at Poynter and a very old e-mail address. WhoWhere does a good job of finding similar names so if you are a bit uncertain of spellings or nicknames, this can help.
- Internet Address Finder: *http://www.iaf.net* The addition of the date of last update to the records you find for a name is helpful. This one found my Poynter address as well as an old address. IAF has over 6,700,000 addresses.
- Yahoo! People Search: *http://people.yahoo.com* You can designate domain, city, state, and country as well as search by name. They found three e-mail addresses for me, my current address, a very old one (Delphi) and a pretty old one (AOL). Oddly enough, though it is affiliated with Yahoo!, it didn't find my Yahoo! mail address.
- InfoSpace: *http://www.infospace.com* In addition to a regular e-mail lookup, InfoSpace also has a "reverse" e-mail lookup. If you just know the e-mail address and want to find who it belongs to, check here. You can also find people who have their e-mail at a particular domain by just typing in the @domain.name. Infospace only found my old e-mail address, but it knew, and stated, that I lived in St. Petersburg, FL.
- Usenet Addresses: *http://usenet-addresses.mit.edu* A directory of over 4,000,000 e-mail addresses compiled from postings to Usenet (newsgroups). They had my current address (and the date that I posted to a newsgroup).
- PeopleSearch: *http://peoplesearch.net* PeopleSearch takes your search and sends it out to 10 e-mail and phone directories. (It spawns a new browser for each one, so it's sort of messy.)

- MESA: Meta Email Search Agent: *http:mesa.rrzn.uni-hannover.de* Searches 6 e-mail databases in one search. Worldwide coverage.

International E-Mail Directories

- World E-Mail Directory: *http://www.worldemail.com/wede4e.shtml* Divided into continents and then by country, many of the e-mail directories have the search box right on this compilation page.
- Infobel: *http://www.infobel.be/internet/email.asp* The pull-down box lets you select in which country you want to look for e-mail.
- Many countries have individual e-mail directories. One technique for finding them is to use a search service, like Infoseek, and search for "e-mail directory" and the name of the country.

Specific E-Mail Directories

If you are looking for the e-mail address of a particular person or would like to contact someone from a specific company, university, agency look for individual e-mail directories or sections on a Web site with a list of e-mail contacts. If you know, for example, the person you are looking for was a graduate of a particular college, see if there is an alumni e-mail directory on the college site. If the person you want is a government official, use one of the government e-mail directories (like the Congressional E-Mail Directory at *http://www.webslingerz.com/jhoffman/congress-email.html* or look at that agency's or branch's Web site.

Free E-Mail Services

In the growing trend to be all things to all Net users, many Web sites offer free e-mail service. These can be useful if you frequently travel and can get Internet access but have trouble getting behind your company's computer firewall to get your office e-mail. I have my office e-mail automatically forwarded to my Yahoo! Mail account when I'm on the road.

They are also a good idea because you can have your office e-mail for official business and a free e-mail account for personal correspondence.

The only trouble with some of these free services is coming up with a user name that hasn't already been used! Try a combination of your regular user name and a series of numbers, that often will do it.

Another problem with some free e-mail services is that you get "spammed" (unsolicited, widely broadcast messages often about a product or service – usually sex-related – you aren't particularly interested in). I dropped my Hotmail account for that reason.

Here are some free e-mail services on the Web. But there are more available every day:

- Yahoo!: *http://mail.yahoo.com* Yahoo! The first directory of the Web and now one of the most wide-ranging portals, offers this free e-mail with lots of features.
- My Own Email: *http://www.myownemail.com* Let's you pick one of 200 domain names for your address.
- RocketMail: *http://www.rocketmail.com*
- Free Email Address Directory: *http://www.emailaddresses.com* Listing of over 700 free email services.

EXERCISES

- Check all of the general e-mail directories listed above and see where, or if, your e-mail address is listed. (Now, go ahead, and try to find that old boyfriend or girlfriend, no one's looking.)
- It's the day after the massacre at Littleton, CO. You'd like to talk with some past students of the high school to see if cliques were a problem in the past. Find the e-mail addresses of a few past or current students of Columbine High School in Littleton, CO.
- There's a new tuition hike at Harvard University which will make it the most expensive school in the world. Find the e-mail addresses of some Harvard students you could contact for comment.
- Find an e-mail directory for Poland.
- What is the e-mail address for a senator from Florida?
- You get an e-mail message with "FW: Fwd: Virus Warning" in the subject line. The message warns you not to open or even look at e-mail that says "Returned or unable to Deliver" because it contains a virus. It urges you to pass this warning on your friends. What do you do?
- Try signing up for one of the free e-mail accounts.

DISCUSSION LISTS

Discussion lists (aka mailing lists and listservs), along with newsgroups, are two ways to join into discussion with other people interested in a particular topic. While newsgroups are modeled after bulletin board message areas, discussion lists are an e-mail routing list. Discussion list software manages the subscription list of those who want to be part of a discussion list. When anyone sends a message to the discussion list, the software sees that a copy is routed to all the members of the discussion list.

Discussion lists can be "open" (anyone who wants can "subscribe"), or "closed" (you must prove you have the necessary credentials – usually job or experience – to belong to the discussion list). Some discussion lists are set up just for members of a committee to correspond, for people from the same organization, or for students taking a particular class.

There are two types of discussion lists: "Moderated" discussion lists generally have a person who looks over messages posted to the list, ensuring that the message is on topic for that particular discussion list's discussion interest. "Unmoderated" discussion lists just pass along anything sent, sometimes resulting in a lot of "noise" (irrelevant messages) on the discussion list.

Another difference between discussion lists and newsgroups is that a newsgroup's membership is more transient, while the discussion list community is fairly constant. Discussion lists are more for personal/professional support and updating while the newsgroups' messages are more for keeping an ear to the ground on a topic or beat.

Discussion lists in reporting and research

There are thousands upon thousands of discussion lists dealing from very specific to more general discussion. For example, look for discussion lists on the topic "crime" and you'll find one specifically for discussion of the

SOURCES

ONLINE RESOURCES/ARTICLES:

"The Digital Watercooler gets hot";
Columbia Journalism Review,
01/01/99, pg. 16
*http://www.cjr.org/year/99/1/
discussion.asp*

Discussion lists: The Good News and
the Bad News, by Randall Marcinko.
Searcher Magazine, Nov./Dec. 1998,
pgs. 34-39
*http://www.infotoday.com/searcher/
nov98/marcinko.htm*

National Crime Survey and another for the more general topic of juvenile delinquency.

The number of discussion lists is growing rapidly because of a number of services which let individuals set up discussion groups (in the past people had to have access to discussion list software running on a network). Services, such as eGroups: *http://www.egroups.com* and Topica *http://www.topica.com* have thousands of discussion groups, everything from individual family lists, boy scout troops, to people who want to join together to discuss particular issues. These can be very esoteric, and can be good ways to find people who have had certain kinds of experiences or hold "interesting" opinions on topics.

The people who "subscribe" to discussion lists generally are very knowledgeable and/or interested in the topic of the list either because of their profession or their life experiences. Estimates are that fewer than 15% of the subscribers to a list actively post messages, the rest being "lurkers" (they read but rarely respond). However, all of the subscribers, whether just readers or active participants, have their own personal networks of contacts that might be helpful to you. Posting questions (if they haven't been answered, and re-answered in the past – doing that might get you flamed) to the list can tap you into a group of experts and people with experience. Discussion lists are also often the early warning system for events and trends being spotted by a group of people with a great deal of interest in a topic.

Anyone with a specific "beat" (health or education or environment, for example) should subscribe to at least one discussion list on that topic. This is a great way to keep up with what experts are talking about, solicit information, advice or contacts from them and to generally tap into a broad expert base.

One of the great journalist resources combines e-mail messaging and discussion lists. **Profnet:** *http://www.profnet.com* is a discussion list set-up for college and university public relations staff. Journalists can send an e-mail message to *profnet@profnet.com,* call *1-800-PROFNET (1-800-776-3638)* (or outside U.S. or Canada: *516-941-3736),* send a fax to *516-689-1425* or submit the request from the Web site at *http://www.profnet.com.* Profnet will post it to the Profnet discussion list. The subscribers (the PR staff) read these messages requesting contacts with experts in universities and put the journalist in touch with appropriate faculty members.

There is a similar service for U.K. universities called Expert Net: *http://www.cvcp.ac.uk/What_We_Do/ExpertNet/expertnet.html*

Other uses

- **Keep in touch with colleagues:** There are numerous discussion lists for journalists. Whether you are a copyeditor, a news researcher, a computer-assisted reporting specialist, or a photojournalist, there is a discussion list of your colleagues. See Barbara Croll Fought's The Newhouse Net List #1: Internet Mailing Lists about Public Communications at *http://web.syr.edu/~bcfought/nnl1.html* for a nicely organized and up-to-date list of journalism related lists.
- **Request information, raise concerns:** As a professional development tool, these communities are great support groups. Discussion lists you might join because of beat responsibilities can help you stay up on the latest interests and concerns of the members of that discussion list.

- **Receive e-zines:** Hundreds of specialty publications are distributed only through discussion list subscriptions. Search John Labovitz's E*Zine*List: *http://www.meer.net/~johnl/e-zine-list/index.html* with more than 3700 titles, to find some that may be useful. The E-Text Archives: *http://www.etext.org* is a searchable database of articles from e-zines that have alternative viewpoints.
- **Alert Services**: Many alert services operate as discussion lists. Sign up to various government agency services and get the latest news releases sent to your e-mail box. See the section on alert services for more information, pp. 53-58.

Discussion list anecdotes

- Mark Schleifstein, reporter at *The Times-Picayune* in New Orleans: *For our series, "Home Wreckers: How the Formosan Termite Devastated New Orleans", we used discussion lists extensively to find and query entomologists around the world. I found ENT-CHN, a discussion list for entomologists of Chinese descent that allowed me to contact scientists in mainland China who had done research on the termite and were able to give me up-to-date information on the damage they caused in southern China.*

  Whenever I begin a new project or know I will be writing several stories on a topic, I'll search out discussion lists that are on point and begin lurking to find sources and up-to-date information.

  During a recent controversy concerning the Tulane Environmental Law Clinic and Supreme Court changes to rules governing who clinic students can represent, I found LAWCLINIC, a discussion list for clinic professors. It was invaluable in tracking down critics of the policy. It was also where I first found out that the present director of the Tulane environmental clinic was resigning.
- Liisa Tuominen, news researcher at the *Ottawa Citizen: Way back in 1994 we used Profnet for the first time. A reporter was doing a story on karaoke and we found, through Profnet, within 24 hours, someone who was doing his PhD dissertation on karaoke. He was a great source that we NEVER would have found otherwise.*
- Anne Winthrop Esposito, magazine writer: *I subscribe to several discussion lists. Some of them, such as MagWrite and Cyber-Hacks, are great for tips, support, inside information, and writing critiques.*
- Carole Ashkinaze, writer-editor: *When my hard-drive crashed, I lost dozens of search engines, and links to hundreds of sites, which were as valuable to me as my old desk-top Rolodex was in the old days. In desperation, I turned to my favorite discussion list (CARR-L) for help, and within hours had enough links and engines to go back to work – and detailed instructions for backing up my bookmarked sites to keep from losing them if it happens again. The List really saved my butt.*

What you need to use discussion lists

One of the great things about discussion lists is they are useful even to those with lower-end equipment. As long as you have an Internet e-mail address you can join a discussion list.

Cost

Most discussion lists are free to belong to, a few request a subscription fee to join. (Caveat: Be careful when reading over your Internet service's charges if you are on a subscription account. Sometimes there are additional charges for numbers of e-mail messages received or amount of storage of messages. This could add up if you belong to a very active discussion list.)

Instructions for using discussion lists

There are two different addresses for discussion lists. One is the administrative address, the address of the discussion list software. This is used for all the administrative functions (subscribe, unsubscribe, hold messages, etc.). Some of the usual software names that you'll see in the administrative address are LISTSERV or LISTPROC or MAJORDOMO.

The other address is the discussion list address of the specific list you want to be part of. Discussion list software, sitting on a computer somewhere, might be maintaining a number of different discussion lists. Everyone would send administrative instructions to that software's administrative address and then specify the discussion list they were interested in in the message. Discussion list addresses look like e-mail addresses and the administrative and discussion list addresses differ only in the part before the @ sign, the domain name is the same.

To subscribe to a list

Send an e-mail message to the discussion list's administrative address with one line in the body of the message: (subscribe listname yourname) where listname is the name of the list, and yourname is your full name (i.e., subscribe CARR-L Jane Smith). When your "subscription" goes through, you will be sent a message with instructions for posting and unsubscribing from the list. Keep these instructions, they will help you get the most out of your discussion list subscription.

Sending a message to the list

Send messages to the discussion list address, the one with the specific discussion list name before the @ sign. Be very careful not to send administrative instructions to the discussion list address, only send them to the administrative address.

Tips and traps when using discussion lists

- **Flame-prone lists:** Some discussion list groups are, frankly, friendlier than others. "Lurk" for awhile (read messages but don't send messages) to get a feel for the tone of that particular discussion list. Also, always read the directions for how to post to the list and how to "unsubscribe", nothing generates more irate messages than uninformed users. Getting flamed (curt or cutting messages about your posting) can keep you from getting fully involved in the group. Part of being on a list is knowing that list's style.
- **Stay on topic/know what's been discussed:** Other instant sources of flamebait, people who wander off the topic of the list's discussion or who bring up a topic that has been discussed to death. Check the archives of the discussion lists messages or find the FAQ (frequently asked questions) document to see if topics you want to bring up have been covered.
- **Consider the source of the message:** One of the benefits of discussion lists over newsgroups is the stability of the user base. Some discussion lists restrict members to those who have a legitimate in-

terest or knowledge in the topic being discussed (closed lists). So, although it is often easier to confirm the legitimacy of the members of a list, it is still important to verify anything posted to a list.

- **Don't quote without permission:** Consider e-mail messages the same as you would personal correspondence or telephone conversations. If you are going to quote, let the speaker (typist) know.

- **Don't use on deadline:** Don't expect to post a message to a list (or a newsgroup) and get an immediate response. If you are on deadline, this may not be the technique to try.

- **Identify yourself:** The messages get posted to the list and look as if they come from the list, not from an individual, so be sure you add your "sig" to any message so readers can readily identify who sent it.

- **Be generous:** What goes around, comes around. If you've gotten help or advice from people on the list, be sure to be an active participant and help out others. The quality of the discussion depends on the individual members.

- **DON'T SHOUT:** A message typed in all caps looks like shouting in the world of discussion lists. Be sure you don't have caps lock on, and try emphasis by putting an asterisk on either side of the word.

- **Re-read before you post:** The ease and quickness of e-mailing messages to lists can sometimes be dangerous. Be sure to look over what you post before you send it – messages live a long time in cyberspace, and you never know just who will be reading the message.

- **Beware the over-flowing e-mail box:** Some discussion lists might generate dozens of messages a day. If you don't monitor your e-mail box regularly, you could quickly be overwhelmed with messages. Some discussion lists provide a "digest" feature which merges all the messages sent to the list and sends out just one huge message to your mailbox a day. This can cut down on the message volume.

- **Pick your group carefully:** Make sure the community you are joining is the right one for you. You will be getting lots of e-mail, so if you find that most is irrelevant or annoying, it will only be taking up your time.

- **Don't advertise:** Most discussion list subscribers deeply resent being used as a promotions mailing list. Unless the group specifically allows advertising type announcements, don't send them.

- **If it's personal, send it to a person:** Be sure to send messages that might have limited interest to specific people rather than to the discussion list.

- **Ask for help if you need it, not just because you're lazy:** Sure, you can post to an astronomy discussion list and ask for an explanation of the "big bang", but you will probably get flamed. If you can look it up, don't expect the members of the discussion list to waste their time responding. And don't send out 25 question surveys to a list, at the very worst you'll just be ignored.

Bill Ruberry, training and technology director at the *Richmond Times-Dispatch,* has these additional tips for effective, and safe, use of discussion lists:

- Avoid embarrassment by taking care in replying to messages or posts. You could unwittingly send a communication intended for one person to an entire mailing list or newsgroup. Automatic replies typically go back to the address that originated the post – in many cases,

SOURCES

List Etiquette: the List member's
guide to E-mail List guidelines,
Rules and Behavior:
http://List-Etiquette.com

a list or group. It's often best to type in the address instead of relying on the "reply" button.

- When publicly replying to a message, summarize the original message or copy enough of it into your response so other readers will understand the context. But don't copy the whole thing. This wastes network capacity, or bandwidth.
- Do not cross-post the same message on many newsgroups or mailing lists unless it is clearly appropriate.
- If you discover an error in your post, correct it as soon as possible.
- If you post a question, be sure to follow up later with a summary of the replies.
- If a message is more than 100 lines long, alert readers by putting the word "Long" in the subject header.
- Avoid "me too" messages. Merely agreeing with a post without offering a new idea is frowned upon.
- Make messages reasonably brief and to the point. Rambling is a no-no.

How to find discussion lists/instructions for using discussion lists

When using directories of discussion lists remember what it is you are searching. Directory databases contain only a minimum amount of information about the discussion list: name, a brief description, and, possibly, some keywords. You are not searching the actual content of the messages posted to the discussion list. So, keep your search general, you'll be more likely to find references to relevant discussion lists than if you get too specific.

If you are working on a project about racial discrimination in the workplace, don't search for those words exactly, you might find "workplace" or "race relations". When you've identified some discussion lists in which members might be discussing that sort of topic, then you can subscribe and post messages looking for comment on the more specific topic.

Be sure to read the help file on the directory site to find out more about search functions. Some directories, for example, ignore punctuation so if you look for that great CARR-L discussion list address by typing in CARR-L, it won't be found. Just type in CARR or put in Computer-Assisted Reporting.

Some directories have two ways to locate discussion lists, a general search which looks for words anywhere in the entry, and a browsable alphabetical list to look up lists by their name.

When you've located a list that looks like it might be interesting, send a message to the list "owner" (the person who either started or maintains the list) to get more information about the kinds of things that are discussed and, if you have concerns, whether or not journalists would be welcome as part of the group.

- Liszt: *http://www.liszt.com*

Liszt has a database with information on over 90,000 mailing lists. There are two ways to find lists listed in Liszt, search the database or look in the Yahoo-esque subject directory. There is a "junk" filter feature which lets you screen out lists intended only for people in a particular organization or attending a class. If you do a search in Liszt mailing lists, it automatically puts that search into the newsgroup and chat search boxes, too, for easy location of all kinds of discussions on the Internet.

- Tile.net : *http://tile.net/lists/*

TILE.NET "The reference to Internet Discussion and Information Lists" contains indexes to discussion lists grouped by description, name, and domain. Click on one you are interested in to get a full description of the discussion list, who can join, where it is, subscription address and administrator's address.

- Directory of Scholarly and Professional E-Conferences: *http://www. n2h2.com/KOVACS/*

This directory includes discussion lists and newsgroups which have been evaluated and determined to be of interest to those with professional or scholarly interests. The entries for each item include the name, a short description, the administrative address, whether the list is moderated, if there are archives of messages, owner contact address, submission address, and keywords. This site is a good one to go to if you just want to join discussions which will be reasonably intellectual.

- Publicly Accessible Mailing Lists: *http://www.neosoft.com/internet/paml*

The help file is very clear and the listing of hits gives you some description of the discussion lists to help you decide which one might be useful. The entry includes the full description of the discussion list, contact name, addresses and when the entry was last checked.

- TOPICA: *http://www.topica.com*

Topica's newly expanded service includes a search of the Discussion List Databases from Liszt, PAML, and Tile.net.

A quick comparison

I looked for lists discussing "managed care" issues and found the following:

- **Liszt:** Found six: amso-letter (a zine on managed care topics), dialog (plaintiff's views of managed care organizations), MBHC (managed behavioral health care), MCAREDIS (managed care and disabilities), MGCMD (managed care clinic MDs discussion), PQE UNM-L (UNM/Lovelace Medicaid managed care).
- **Tile.net:** Found one, MHCARE-L (Managed Health Care Discussion Forum)
- **Topica:** Found six; three from Liszt, three new ones: Families USAMC (a newsletter), Nuts 'n Bolts of starting a private practice, and Ped Talk (pediatric discussions).
- **Publicly Accessible Mailing Lists:** Found 2 – Health, Risk and Society (a peer-reviewed journal which sends it's table of contents to subscribers of the list), and Psych_Pract (a discussion list for general public and psychologists/psychotherapists).
- **Directory of Scholarly and Professional E-Conferences:** Found 2 – CINMHC (discussion of California related health care issues), and NHCTEN (discussion of the evaluation of managed care initiatives).

As you can see, none of the five different directories found the same discussion lists, only a few of the discussion lists were found in more than one directory. You can also see the very specific focus of some of these lists (and if I were a reporter covering managed care I'd sure find the discussion between managed care clinic MDs mighty interesting).

Archives of discussion list messages

It used to be that discussion list messages were accessible only to those who subscribed to the list. Discussion list subscribers could send a command to the list to perform a search of messages sent to the discussion list and any that matched the keywords would be delivered in an e-mail message.

For specific instructions for searching archived messages see:

- Listserv software: *http://www.lsoft.com/manuals/1.8d/user/user. html#3.3*
- Majordomo software: *http://www.dipoli.hut.fi/org/TechNet/org/ humanities/news-help/message_archives.html*
- Or try this e-mail archive search form: *http://stripe.colorado.edu/ ~itrc/listsearch.html*

Now there are ways to check messages posted to discussion lists you haven't subscribed to. A service called Reference.com: *http://www.reference.com* claims to be maintaining an archive of discussion list (and newsgroup) messages. (However, they have had intermittent server problems, and the search often is not working).

The "make your own" discussion list service, eGroups: *http://www. egroups.com*, keeps an archive of past messages by month for the groups on their service. This is also a nice service because it tells you how many members there are, and how many messages have been posted to the group.

Topica: *http://www.topica.com* has a search box where you can enter words to find either discussion lists on that topic or messages which contain that word from discussion lists hosted on Topica.

The archiving of discussion list messages is something to watch. These could be valuable resources for locating certain types of people. But it is also important to keep in mind that you might possibly have the words you type to your discussion list community available for others to see.

Exercises

- The newsroom is gearing up for the 2000 Census. Find some discussion lists that might be useful in building contacts lists, receiving bulletins, getting story angles.
- A new treatment for Parkinson's disease has been announced. Find a few messages about Parkinson's disease.
- You've just been named your paper's cops reporter, a new beat for you. Find a discussion list that would have colleagues you should bond with.
- You're a TV reporter and just heard about a zine that is supposed to be pretty interesting, called the Electronic Broadcaster. How can you subscribe to it?
- Looks like Al Gore is going to run for President. You've been keeping up with the mainstream press but what has the zine press been saying about him? Find some articles from zines that mention Gore.
- Now, think of your favorite hobby and find a group you'd like to join into discussion with on that hobby or interest, and go sign on!

NEWSGROUPS AND FORUMS

Discussion lists are one of several ways you can read or take part in discussions between individuals on the Internet. Another is to join a chat session. But one of the most popular ways is to join a newsgroup. The main difference between these methods are that you sign-up for a discussion list and the messages go to your e-mail box, you go into a chatroom and see the conversation in "real-time", while you go to a newsgroup area and read the messages like a bulletin board.

Newsgroups are actually the collection of "articles" (messages) distributed through Usenet, a system developed to pass messages from one network to another (rather than to individuals). The newsgroups are the subject organization of these Usenet messages.

Forums are like newsgroups but they are generally found as a feature within a Web site. An individual Web site will host various forums for its users to allow them to post comments, raise issues and get group support.

Newsgroup and forum messages are posted publicly, available for anyone to read and respond to. There are more than 80,000 discussion areas (up from the 15,000 estimated in the last edition) currently active on the Internet covering every conceivable topic from the arts to zoology.

Newsgroups and forums in reporting and research

- **Story ideas:** While some of the messages will be more like CB radio talk, others can give you a first alert about a developing new topic or area of concern to the group. You can get leads and angles on a story you are working on. Browsing newsgroups of interest to see what topics really have people going (lots of messages being posted about a particular topic) can be a good tip to a likely interesting story.
- **Finding sources to talk to:** The people who read newsgroup messages are a great source for information themselves, and they know others who are experts or experienced in the topic being discussed. By connecting to a newsgroup's population, you are connecting to their rolodexes, too.
- **Seeking people who know about a specific topic:** Again, anyone who joins a newsgroup is likely to be very interested, concerned or knowledgeable about the topic being discussed. The group is highly motivated to share information and answer questions raised by other members.
- **Find people it might be hard to find otherwise:** Doing a story on impotence and the impact (and problems) with Viagra use? How would you find people who wanted to talk about it or get an idea of the problems they have had? Go to alt.personals.viagra-users! People getting support in a newsgroup for diseases or personal situations that might be hard to find can be located in newsgroups. Each of the more than 80 diseases and medical conditions listed at MediConsult: *http://www.mediconsult.com* has a support group link to a forum where people are discussing their experiences with the disease.
- **Get good backgrounders:** Most newsgroups have compiled FAQs (frequently asked questions) for their topic area. These often answer the basic sorts of background questions you might have when needing to get up to speed on a topic. Find FAQs from Usenet newsgroups at Usenet FAQs: *http://www.cis.ohio-state.edu/hypertext/faq/usenet/FAQ-List.html* or Internet FAQ Archives: *http://www.faqs.org/faqs/*

SOURCES

BOOKS

Rittner's Field Guide to Usenet, by Don Rittner. MNS, 1997

Netizens : On the History and Impact of Usenet and the Internet, by Michael Huben, Ronda Hauden. IEEE Computer Society, 1997

ARTICLES

Sleuthing Usenet Newsgroups: One newspaper's digital investigation, by David Noack, E&P Interactive, July 18, 1997 *http://www.mediainfo.com/ephome/news/newshtm/stories/071897n1.htm*

■ **Find key articles and esoteric documents:** Newsgroup members frequently post articles and reports they have found and that they think will interest others. You can sometimes find articles that you might have had to go into a subscription site to get. (Of course, copyright is a whole 'nother issue that we won't get into here.)

■ **Your news organization's Web site:** The forums hosted by your news Web site can be valuable resources in your reporting. Check the comments and complaints about news stories that have been covered and you'll often get sources or story ideas.

Newsgroup and forum anecdotes

Jim Krane, reporter at APBonline *http://www.apbonline.com : I was doing an unrelated newsgroup search (looking for info on the U.S. vs. Microsoft case) when I stumbled across a newsgroup called Russian and Eastern European Brides. I downloaded a few hundred messages and began looking them over. The purpose of the newsgroup was to give (usually older) Western men tips on meeting and marrying (usually young) women from Russia, the Ukraine and other Eastern European countries.*

In the midst of this how-to discussion was a post titled something like: "Danger: My Father was Murdered by a Catalog Bride." The posting was written by a woman in Texas. Her story about her 64-year-old father marrying – and then allegedly being murdered by – a 24-year-old Ukrainian woman, sounded compelling.

I phoned the woman and ended up in a weeks long investigation involving investigators, witnesses, and the prime suspects in Odessa, Ukraine where her father had died. I got death certificates, marriage certificate, wedding photos and a hand-written note from the murdered man imploring all readers to "Investigate my death." He wrote that he believed his wife would kill him. My stories on the case were translated and ran in Ukrainian newspapers where they put pressure on investigators to re-open a closed case. An arrest is now imminent. (See the story resulting from this serendipitous newsgroup find at http://www.apbonline.com/indepth/bride.html)

From participants in a Producing New Media seminar at Poynter (these were the folks that work on the Web site):

● *When some police officers were shot in Phoenix, the letters of condolence written to our forum on the topic gave the reporters some material for their story.*

● *During a recent gas price hike we put up a forum on where to find the cheapest gas in town. This provided a sidebar to the main piece on the gas prices. We have a genealogy forum on our Web site and there is a reporter at the paper who does a column each week using questions and comments from that forum.*

What you need to use newsgroups and forums

Newsgroups are the subject collection of articles distributed through Usenet. In the past, the network or service you used for Internet access had to have the Usenet mail reader software loaded, and the newsgroups you wanted to read had to be "subscribed" to.

But now, anyone can get newsgroup message access through a Web site which collects and compiles and archives newsgroup messages called

Deja (more about Deja, formerly known as DejaNews, below in the section on Finding Newsgroups and Forums).

Forums are found on individual Web sites so, to get access to forums, all you need is your browser and access to the Web.

Cost

The service you use for Internet access might charge by the hour for the time you spend reading messages. Otherwise, there is no fee for reading newsgroup messages or for joining newsgroup discussions. Some forum areas might be restricted to subscribers to the Web site if the Web site is one that requires a subscription.

Tips and traps when using newsgroups and forums

Newsgroups and forums are great resources for connecting with experts and people with certain types of experiences. However, there are some things you should keep in mind as you are using them:

- **You need lead time:** You might post a message and not get a response for a day or two. Don't rely on responses for short deadline stories.
- **Identify yourself:** Although you're in cyberspace, you need the same ethics as when you're dealing with people face to face. If you are trolling for comments to use in a story, be sure to disclose who you are and something about why you are looking for comments.
- **Remember, what you post will be read by who knows who:** Don't tip your hand on a big story, there may be other journalists out there. Be as vague as possible but specific enough to get some response. Ask people to reply to your e-mail address, not to post to the newsgroup.
- **Verify, verify, verify:** Would you put in the paper something you heard at a cocktail party without verifying it? Of course not. Same with what you read in a newsgroup.
- **Read the FAQs:** Don't become instant flamebait (the target of vitriolic messages by other members) by asking a question that has already been answered by the group. Be sure to find and read the FAQ (frequently asked questions) document which most newsgroups have available on their topic.
- **Search the Archive:** Many newsgroups retain an archive of messages. Before you send out a question, search to see if it has already been addressed by the group. (A source for locating newsgroup archives can be found at: *http://starbase.neosoft.com/~claird/ news.lists/newsgroup_archives.html*)
- **Get a sense of the climate before you get active:** Lurk (read messages but don't send or reply) for awhile on the newsgroup before you become active. Learn about the community of people, their concerns, their tolerance level before you solicit information from them. Be as sensitive to the group as you would be in a face-to-face situation. And don't overdo it. When Jerry Garcia died, a message was posted by a journalist to the rec.music.gdead newsgroup, asking for stories or memories anyone would like to share, information about local vigils, etc. One member of the newsgroup responded, "You want a comment? How about "GO THE F*** AWAY! You can read the posts here. People are upset. Stop digging for news bites and let us

grieve!" Bottom line: this is a great resource for journalists, just be sure to use it appropriately and sensitively.

- **Find a few to monitor:** As with all the Internet resources, if you start off thinking you have to eat the whole thing, you will quickly have a stomachache. Take small bites, find a few good places, monitor them well, and build up your skills. Get this technique for covering your beat incorporated into your style of work.

- **If there is a choice between a moderated and an unmoderated newsgroup on a topic, go moderated:** Moderated lists usually have someone who oversees the message traffic to see that it stays on topic and to mediate flamewars. Unmoderated are "anything goes", and what often goes is trivial, off-point kinds of messages. Most newsgroup lists and finders will indicate whether or not a newsgroup is moderated.

- **Remember the audience:** This, more than any other use of the Internet, is the most problematic in terms of verifying the source of the information, determining their agenda. This is truly unfiltered information and should be used carefully. Depending on the kind of story you are doing, this can be a great source. When rumors were rampant about an errant military jet pilot who disappeared over Colorado, newsgroups were a great place to go to read the crazy theories for a story on crazy theories. These are the bar rooms, locker rooms and living rooms of the Internet.

How to find newsgroups and forums

The hierarchy of Usenet newsgroups is eight main areas, regulated by Usenet, and hundreds of other areas which anyone can start up. The main eight are:

Biz	Business-related topics
Comp	Computer-related topics
Misc	Miscellaneous topics
News	Current events
Rec	Recreation and entertainment
Sci	Science
Soc	Society and culture
Talk	Discussion and debate on many topics

The largest and most wide ranging newsgroup is alt: for alternative. Here's where you will find all the fan newsgroups and bizarre interest areas.

Newsgroup names are a series of letters and words separated by periods. For example: soc.culture.african.

Forums are discussion areas found in various Web sites and on different Web services (like AOL). They might be called the Bulletin Board or Feedback. Getting into a forum area often requires a registration (they want to keep track of who has come onto their service). These are generally a more controlled community. If you are looking for people who might be talking about a topic you are interested in, check with the major Web sites for that topic area. Chances are excellent that one or more will have some sort of discussion area on the site.

If, for example, you are interested in issues going on in a particular part of the country, go to the local newspaper site and read the discussion area postings to get some insights (though don't be surprised if the thing people seem to be most agitated about are the local sports team!)

These forum/discussion/bulletin board areas are often hidden down in the site, so it can take some looking to find them.

Various services archive newsgroup messages and help you locate forums and newsgroups where people are discussing certain topics:

Deja: *http://www.deja.com*

This is definitely the best of the newsgroup directory/archive services. Deja tracks information about more than 80,000 newsgroups and forums. They also have the most extensive archive of individual messages posted to more than 45,000 newsgroups. The archive of messages goes back to 1995.

Deja changed it's name from DejaNews in May 1999, and along with the new name came some new services, some very useful, some just noise.

Finding newsgroups and newsgroup messages on Deja

There are two levels of searching in Deja: simple and advanced.

- **Simple search:** Plug a word in the search box in the upper right hand side of the homepage. Make sure the button next to "Discussions" is selected. ("Ratings" are Deja's flaky popularity polls feature. "Communities" are the forums which Deja subscribers can set up.)
- **Power Search:** Click on "Power Search" under the search box and get a search form which lets you type in keywords and designate an "and" or "or" relationships between them. (See the section on searching for more about "boolean" connectors.) You can select which of five archives you want to search in: complete, standard, adult, jobs, for sale. You can also search in particular fields: subject of the message, forum name, author of the message. You can look for messages in particular languages or between certain dates in power search.
- **Be aware:** There are two archives of messages, recent and past. When you do a search from the simple or power search templates, you are searching the recent message archive. When you have searched and pulled up the message results list, be sure to go down to the end of the page and find the search box again. The search you just did will be in the search box. Underneath are two buttons, recent and past messages. If you want to find the older messages, click the "past messages" button and re-submit your search. Recent messages cover the past 30 days postings, past messages date back to 1995. I did a search on "mastiffs" and got 137 recent messages. Re-doing the search in past messages got me another 2,200 matches.
- When reading old messages, be aware that the e-mail addresses of posters might have changed. Fresh messages might be better if you are looking for people to contact.

Reading the results page

At the top of the results page is a list of newsgroups where the search term you entered is likely to be discussed. Click on "Get more forums related to…" to get the whole list. Results are ranked by "confidence" (the more + signs, the higher the likelihood your topic is discussed on that forum/newsgroup). If you want to see recent messages posted, click on the newsgroup name. This is a good technique if you would like to see what people are discussing or to locate a likely group which might respond to a message from you on a particular subject.

Underneath the newsgroup listing is a list of messages which contain the search term you used. These will come from a variety of newsgroups (some of which were not on the listing of newsgroups at the top of the page).

You'll get a listing of messages in reverse chronological order (most recent first). This is a good technique if you want to find people who have commented about a topic or would like to browse through messages on a topic to get story angles and ideas.

Categories

Deja has a subject directory of newsgroups that can be used to find appropriate groups to browse. The broad subjects are listed down the left margin. Click on one of those subjects and you'll get a page. Scroll to the end of the page to see a more specific subject directory. Just click on a subject and you'll get a search box which will let you narrow the search you do to newsgroups appropriate to that category.

Reading the messages

Once you've located some messages or found a newsgroup there are various things you can do:

See the "thread": The message thread is the flow of messages on a particular subject. When you click on a message, you'll get a diagram of this message flow. If you want to start at the top of the thread, click on Msg 1.

A great new feature Deja added is "Track this thread for me". If there is an interesting discussion going on and you would like to know when new messages in the thread are posted, click on this. You have to be a registered user of Deja (it's free, just fill out the form). Name the thread you want to track and when new messages are posted, you'll get a copy in your e-mail box.

Read the message: Click on the underlined message to get the text. When you pull up a message you'll get the following information: Author of the message, date it was posted, the forum it was posted to. In the text of the message you'll sometimes see > or >> marks in front of lines. These indicate they are a copy of lines from a previous message to which the writer is responding. The RE: in the subject line of a message indicates the message is a reply to another message.

Get the next or previous message: To scroll the messages in a thread or on the list of messages retrieved for your search, hit the "next in thread" or "previous in thread" arrow in the top right corner.

Reply: There are two options for replying to a message. If you hit the "post reply" button you'll get a template to fill out a message which will be posted to the whole newsgroup. This will be a public posting of the message. If you want to send a personal reply directly to the author of the message, click on the e-mail address in the Author part of the message. If you can't send e-mail from your browser (many companies don't allow that), just copy the author's e-mail address and send a message from your e-mail system. Most journalists do their correspondence with an interesting messager off the newsgroup, through e-mail.

Author Posting History: You see an intriguing message from someone and might want to contact him or her for an interview. Check out other things he or she has posted by clicking on "Posting History". It will give you a listing of the number of messages posted in various forums. Click on the forum name to see the messages. Just seeing the listing of the forums a person is involved in can provide interesting insights.

Deja is the newsgroup directory/archive you'll want to get to know the best. It is the gateway into a vast and varied resource for journalists.

Other Newsgroup/Forum finders

The major search services all have an option for looking for newsgroup messages, but most of them (Infoseek, HotBot) are just using Deja.

- AltaVista: *http://www.altavista.com* – Click on "Usenet" under the "Specialty Searches" area to get a search box for locating newsgroup messages. Results are in chronological order.
- Liszt: *http://www.liszt.com* – Liszt has a directory of 30,000 newsgroups, click on Usenet Newsgroups Directory from the homepage or go to *http://www.liszt.com/news*. Remember this is not finding messages but newsgroup names.
- ForumOne: *http://www.forumone.com* – Over 310,000 Web forum discussions located on individual Web sites. Do a search and get a listing of forum areas discussing that topic. Many forum areas require registration on the site sponsoring that discussion, so it might be a couple of steps to get to the messages themselves.

Exercises

- After another traffic death involving air bags, you are going to do a story covering the issue of use of air bags. Find some newsgroup messages to get ideas of issues people are talking about.
- You're going to be doing a series on domestic violence. Find forums where this is being discussed.
- Find some messages I posted to newsgroups (my e-mail address is npaul@poynter.org). It's been awhile since I've posted.
- You've just gotten a job at the *Miami Herald* and would like to know about the issues that have people talking there. How would you find that out on a forum?
- A member of your family has been diagnosed with Parkinson's disease. Find a support group for him.
- You're getting ready to interview a successful dog breeder. Where might you find some of the kinds of questions that might be good to ask her?

CHAT

Chat rooms, along with e-mailing, discussion lists, newsgroups and forums, are another way to connect with people and their raw (sometimes very raw), unfiltered opinions and perspectives.

Other people-connection tools delay the delivery of messages. For example, e-mail or newsgroup messages get sent and might not be read by anyone for awhile.

SOURCES

BOOKS:

IRC and Online Chat, by James Powers, Abacus Software, 1997.

Learn Internet Relay Chat, by Kathryn Toyer, Wordware Publishing, 1998.

OVERVIEWS AND GUIDELINE BOOKS:

Beginner's Guide to Internet Chat: *http://www.download.com/pc/ed/ review/0,357,0-675-1,00.html*

About.com – Chatting Online Guide: *http://chatting.about.com*

Chat rooms, on the other hand, are "real-time" conversations conducted in virtual meeting halls. When you enter a chat room, you can see the messages as they are being typed by others in the chat area, and you can type in an immediate response.

I have a bias against chat room discussions – for the most part I think they are incredibly shallow and a waste of time. They are chaotic. It's hard to follow the threads of conversation going on and it is usually the lowest common denominator of conversation, with lots of short, pointless comments. But, that is now – and if chat matures as quickly as other aspects of the Web, then this is an Internet tool well worth watching. There is budding potential for use by reporters.

Uses of Chat in Reporting and Research

Chat has become one of the favorite features that Web sites offer to pull in users to the site. Many sponsors schedule chats with celebrities or experts. Subject-specific Web sites often have online discussions with prominent people. These virtual Q&A sessions have an advantage over the live speech because the text of the questions and answers are captured.

Journalists can hold virtual interviews by scheduling a meeting in a chat room with a source and the interview can be held there (again, with the advantage of the text capture). Many find that a chat room interview is more free-flowing than conducting an interview via e-mail.

Chat Anecdotes

Jacksonville Times-Union political writer, Dave Roman, conducted chat room debates with candidates in the local city elections. Readers, editors, reporters and candidates all met online to discuss the issues.

Journalist and trainer Pieter Wessels of Australia uses chat to mentor other working journalists – sometimes half way round the world. It gives a more direct and interactive experience than just exchanging e-mailed advice.

Tips and Traps when using chat

Chatters use lots of shortcuts to speed up their communication and to give a sense of tone to their words. They often use "smileys" or "emoticons", little graphics which denote a reaction (smiling, frowning, puzzled…). And they use acronyms, (IMHO – in my humble opinion, TTFN – ta ta for now). Decipher them with these lists:

Acronyms: *http://www.apc.net/ia/scrmaim.htm*

Emoticons: *http://www.apc.net/ia/scrmaim.htm#emot*

What you need to be able to Chat

There are three different ways to get into the chat scene.

The original way to chat was using IRC – Internet Relay Chat. You had to download software like mIRC before you could hook up with and chat to other users. There are more than 44,000 different chat "channels" on the IRC.

You could also download various other chat software programs, freeware (no cost) or shareware (low cost), that let you chat with other users of that particular chat software. You can get a good explanation of chat software and links to various versions at the Beginner's Guide to Internet Chat: *http://www.download.com/pc/ed/review/0,357,0-675-1,00.html*

Finally, you can join the chat areas, or chat rooms, found on many Web sites and most of the major search services (i.e., Yahoo!: *http://www.yahoo.com*). Some sites specialize in chat only (i.e., TalkCity: *http://www.talkcity.com*) and host hundreds of different chat areas. These require no other software than just your Web browser. However, there is often a registration process involved before you can get into the chat areas on a Web site, but it is usually free.

How to find chat areas or chat events

- Liszt: *http://www.liszt.com/chat/* Liszt has directories of IRC chat channels as well as the directories of newsgroups and discussion lists. Type in a word and it will list a number of places where that topic is likely to be discussed.
- Yack: *http://www.yack.com* Look for different live chats and interviews at this directory site. Search for a topic and find upcoming events on it, find upcoming events by date, or click on the "What's on now" button and get a listing of chats happening right now. There is also a pull-down box with a listing of dozens of "event channels" you can check to see what they will be hosting and when.
- About.com – Chatting Online Guide: *http://chatting.about.com* The About library of useful guides to Web resources includes this one on Chatting. There are links to places to get more information and to locate chat areas on the Web. Look in "NetLinks" under Chat – Transcripts and find some of the text from previous chat interviews.

Exercises:

- You're in a chat room and someone types GAL in response to a long and insightful message you sent – should you be insulted?
- You cover health and like to keep an eye out for interesting topics and discussions. See what chat events will be coming up that might be interesting for the health beat.

FILE TRANSFER PROTOCOL

FTP – file transfer protocol, is another of the early techniques for finding and retrieving information from Internet-networked computers. Unlike gopher and telnet which have been largely supplanted by the Web, FTP is still an important way to get large files and programs downloaded and onto your computer.

In the early days, to do an FTP, you had to know the exact IP address of the computer on the Internet where the document or software you wanted was. You had to know the exact directory and file name of the document or software. Then you used the FTP client software to initiate the download. Now, many of the types of information you can FTP from the Internet can be found on Web sites which will automatically do the download. The high access speeds have helped make file downloads much easier than in the past.

Like gopher, FTP is just finding individual documents or files, not the package of information which the Web with its HTTP (hyper-text transfer protocol) delivers. Often, these files are compressed files (a process of taking out spaces and densely packing the document or program for faster transfer). This requires that you then de-compress it (this is also called un-zipping a zipped file).

The search facility for locating FTP files is called Archie (derived from "archive").

Uses of FTP in Reporting and Research

Large datasets, useful software programs and extensive document files can be found and retrieved through FTPing.

Some valuable documents and data have been acquired through FTP and put on to Web pages as a service to Web users. A good example is the download of Uniform Crime Reports – county-level information which was FTPed from the National Archive of Criminal Justice Data and put into usable form on the GeoStat site at *http://fisher.lib.virginia.edu/crime/*

Tips and Traps for Using FTP

Mostly you will be initiating an FTP after locating a good description of the file from a Web page or some other source. Using the FTP search engines for general searching is almost futile. They don't retrieve enough information about a file to tell you what you will be actually downloading. You can get clues about the download from the file name. For example, I did a search on crime in the Archie server at *http://www.wg.omron.co.jp/AA-eng.html* and got these results. The first line was telling where the FTP server existed (in the first one at core.ring.gr.jp – a computer in Japan, you can tell by the "jp" at the end – see a list of country codes in the Appendices). The second line gives the directory and subdirectories where the document or program sits in the computer. The third line is the actual file name where the extension to the file name explains what type of file it is (find information about file extensions on List of File Extensions: *http://www.lib.rochester.edu/multimed/appen.htm)*

Let's see how to decipher this.

> *Host core.ring.gr.jp*
>
> */pub/mac/info-mac/game*
>
> *crime-city.hqx 123K (126840 bytes) Sep 19 1998*

This is some kind of game software for a Macintosh. You can tell from the file extension .hqx that it is a Mac compressed file format.

Depending on the type of file you find and download, there may be different types of software you need to read it. If you initiate an FTP procedure and get a message saying "You have started to download a file of type application…" then you will need a certain kind of "plug-in" to run it. This is a whole 'nother process about which you can read at LearnTheNet: Plug-ins at *http://www.learnthenet.com/english/html/56plugins.htm* and find plug-ins at Browser Watch: *http://browserwatch.internet.com/plug-in.html.*

Finding FTP sites

I'm currently addicted to Tetris, a game I play on my GameBoy (the one I bought so I wouldn't have to share with the kids). I want to get a copy I can load on my laptop. FTP is the solution…

I went to FileWatcher at *http://filewatcher.org* and typed in *tetris*.* (the * after tetris and after the . made this a wildcard search so I could pick up tetris98 or any kind of file extension that might have been used.) I got 20 items back, telling me the address of the FTP site, the directory and subdi-

GOPHER

The warm and fuzzy sounding gopher is actually an early hero of the Internet frontier. Gopher is a client/server software package developed at the University of Minnesota (the Fighting Gophers) that lets you search for files and documents found in Internet-accessible computers around the world. The development of the gopher search was the beginning of easier access to millions of files (text, audio, graphic). It was a vast improvement over the need to have an exact file location and name and FTP (file transfer protocol) a file.

Gopher searches come back as menus of items that match your search.

Although the World Wide Web has subsumed much of the gopher-accessed information, gopher sites can still contain files, reports, transcripts and documents that are not yet incorporated into a WWW site.

Gopher is a "single-element" delivery system in that it indexes and delivers a single file at a time (a text document, an audio file, a photo or graphic).

Veronica (named as a complement to the FTP search tool Archie and standing for "Very Easy Rodent-Oriented Netwide Index to Computerized Archives") is the software developed to search multiple gopher spaces at the same time.

Uses of gopher in reporting and research

Well, frankly, I can't think of many. So much of the gopher content has been made available on Web sites. It might be worth trolling through gopherspace if you are looking for an obscure old document that predates the Web. But you'll find that Web sites you use to locate documents will, if the document exists in a gopher server, connect to that document without you even recognizing that that is where it came from. When you click on a link and get a flat text page then you've probably connected to a document retrieved from a gopher server.

Journalist and Internet trainer Pieter Wessels said in an e-mail message, "When training working journalists to use the Net I have dropped both telnet and Gopher from the curriculum. It's specialist knowledge now."

What you need to do gopher

Just as with telnet and FTP, which used to require the loading of specific software to use them, doing gopher searches required access to specific software. But now, as with telnet and FTP functions, the browser software you use for the World Wide Web has incorporated gopher functions.

You'll notice if you go to a Web site that connects to a gopher server the address you'll see in the status bar at the bottom of the browser starts with *gopher://* – that stuff before the *://* indicates to the browser what kind of protocol to use (*gopher://* or *telnet://* or *ftp://* or *http://* for a hyper-text transfer protocol of Web pages).

Tips and Traps for using gopher

Some of the main problems with gopher searching and retrieving:

- **Where did it come from?** There is no indication in the menu listing who submitted the information or when it was submitted. You have to retrieve the document and look for clues in the document about who compiled the information or how current it is (and that is not always clearly stated in the document). You can sometimes try to decipher the site where the document resides from the gopher address, but that is not always indicative of who submitted the information.

- **Sorry, connection refused by the server...or Unable to locate server:** Gopher holes are unstable and you'll quite often get a message saying a particular server (the host computer) is not accepting connections. It's a case of "so near, and yet so far" – you know the document you may need is sitting there, but you can't get to it. Or some gopher indexes still have references to materials in servers that are no longer connected to the Internet and so the server is not found.

- **Cannot access directory...:** The gopher search may find the article, but the host doesn't allow "outsiders" into the files.

- **Great title, but lousy content:** Sometimes the advance billing doesn't match what you get when you get there. For example, a search for Branch Davidians retrieved the promising sounding: "From life to fiery death: the Branch Davidians and the Federal Government." Click on the link and you get a brief bibliographic citation to a documentary done by Pacific Radio.

Finding Gopher documents

There are a number of sites that help you locate gopher documents although there seem to be fewer and fewer of them in operation. Here is one of the more reliable ones, from Galaxy: *http://galaxy.einet.net/GJ/*

ALERT SERVICES AND FILTERS

**Much of the information about alert services in this chapter comes from Jennifer Small, Assistant Editor of Information Services, *San Antonio Express News*.

E-mail, a tool of the Internet which connects you to primary sources, people, is also a valuable tool for connecting you with secondary sources: reports, documents, updates.

There are two types of service. Alert services found on Web sites (variously known as "watch lists", "distribution lists", "current awareness services") use discussion list software to maintain a list of people interested in updates and news releases which are then sent to their e-mail address. Everyone who subscribes to the alert service receives the same documents or news releases.

Filters, on the other hand, provide customization. They can be used to get news stories from wire services or messages from newsgroups which fit the subject profile you set up. You sign-up and type in words about the types of topics you want the filter to catch. The software stores your interest profile and uses it to check the stories or messages it filters. When it finds a story or message containing the words you have in your profile, the program snags it and posts it to your e-mail box (or an area on the service you can check).

Some alerts notify users when new information or changes have been made to a Web site they are interested in. Others automatically send new information to the subscribers of the alert service.

For years, commercial online services like Lexis-Nexis or Dow Jones have been providing alert and filter services, usually at a very high cost. The free alert services on the Internet are becoming viable alternatives. The tools are not only becoming more advanced, but they are also covering a wider range of topics.

Uses of Alert services in reporting and research

- **Stay on top of your beat:** Find some of the key Web sites useful to your beat. These will often have alert services available. This fresh information will keep you up to speed and aware of new developments.
- **Stay ahead of the competition:** Sign up for the alert service and you will be the first to know about new information released by those sources. This can often provide leads before the rest of the news media have caught on.
- **Make Web use more efficient:** Use of Web site monitoring services can be a time-saver. Set up a service to retrieve specific sections of Web sites and compile them into an easily used package.
- **Find the latest stories on a topic you are covering:** If you are getting ready to do a major investigation or project, create a wire service news filter on the topic you will be writing about. You'll get stories from around the world which relate to the story you will be writing about (great for retrieving background information and for broadening the perspective of your reporting).
- **Find sources, angles, experts:** Looking for sources, people who are interested or knowledgeable about a topic? Use a message news filter and you'll get the messages posted by individuals that contain

the words you are interested in. Individuals can then be contacted through e-mail for more comment.

Alert Service and Filter Anecdotes

A reporter for the *San Antonio Express-News* in the Laredo bureau uses the GAO (General Accounting Office) alert service. He said he used to have to wait for press releases from Washington to get a story and then he'd have to rely on the info that a Press Information Officer provided. With the alert he felt for the first time that he was on top of news because he received notes of released reports and those to come. Then he was able to link to the whole report rather than relying on the bits or pieces that were released from DC.

Heather Newman, computer and technology reporter at the *Detroit Free Press: I've gotten plenty of good ideas from QuickBrowse: http:// www.quickbrowse.com. You specify the Web pages that you want copied and sent to you via email each morning (or however often you'd like). I have all the major front pages from computer news sites online clipped, smooshed together into a single message and sent to me daily at 6 a.m. Then I can scroll through them all, complete with their original graphics and working links, without having to visit each site for info. Our features editor does this with features pages from newspaper sites.*

I also subscribe to news alerts from IDC, Forrester and ProfNet (their Technology news briefs), all of which have provided me with tips and experts for tech coverage.

Tips and Traps when using alert services and filters

- You will need to register to get on an alert service. Your name, affiliation, title, and e-mail address will be requested.
- Many services require you to use a sign-on and password. Keeping track of the sign-on names and passwords you've used for various services can be a problem. Create a rolodex of the services you've subscribed to, you'll need the information if you want to go in and change the profile or unsubscribe.
- Keep in mind that alert service registration lists could be sold or used by others who would want to contact people interested in alerts on a topic. They might be sold to advertisers or others you might not want to have contacting you. Find out the registration list policy of the alert service you are using; you can often opt out of being on a distributable list.
- Don't let your enthusiasm for this type of service overwhelm you. You don't want to set up the e-mail box equivalent of a physical in-box overflowing with press releases and reports you'll never get around to reading.
- Take care when setting up your filters. Some have you choose from pre-selected subject categories, others let you put in your own topics. Creating a profile which is too broad will result in irrelevant hits, one that is too narrow will make you miss stories of possible interest. You'll want to experiment with the terms you use in your profiles.
- Know how the filter works. Some will just match character by character. The keyword "labor" won't find "labour". Others work on a relevancy model where similar words will be caught, too, but given a lower relevance in the results calculation. For example, search for "Eyal" (the name of the radical Israeli group Rabin's assassin be-

longed to) in a relevancy search and it will find articles with "eye" or "eyes" as well.

- Know what the filter is filtering: If you are hoping to be notified of any messages about a new medication posted to alt.support.depression be sure you know if your news filter monitors that area. Deja, for example, doesn't filter messages posted to alt.*, soc.*, talk.* or *.binaries news groups.
- Bottom line – read the FAQ: Virtually every service has a FAQ (frequently asked questions) list which will answer all your questions about how the search engine works, how often the files are searched, how you can modify your search for better results. Take the time to find, and read, the FAQ or user manual – it will save time in the long run.

How to find alert services

Alert services are becoming commonplace on Web sites, particularly on association and government sites. The sorts of organizations that would provide press releases often use alert services as an alternative (and sometimes as the only way to get news releases). As you search the Web for sites with valuable and timely information on a topic you are covering, always pay attention to opportunities to subscribe to alerts or lists on these sites.

You might try using a search site to search for a topic, and for the terms "alert services", "updates", "current awareness" to locate Web sites with those kinds of services.

Following are some examples of alert services for particular beats. Also, check out Bill Dedman's Alert! Page: *http://PowerReporting.com/alert.html* for alert services grouped by 15 different categories.

Alert services by topic

Government

- **White House:** Reporters can automatically receive White House briefings: *http://www.pub.whitehouse.gov/WH/Publications/html/Publications.html#subscribe*.
- **Tracking developments on Capitol Hill:** Subscribe to both the *Whipping Post* and the *Whip Notice: http://majoritywhip.house.gov/mail* The *Post* lists legislation to be considered on a particular day, when votes are expected as well as starting and ending times for the House. The *Notice* is a weekly publication that comes out Friday evenings and summarizes legislation that is expected on the floor the next week.
- **Campaign finance updates:** Political reporters may want to consider alerts provided by organizations outside the federal government. The Center for Responsive Politics: *http://www.opensecrets.org/news/listadd.htm* provides alerts for those tracking campaign contributions.
- **GAO Reports:** The General Accounting Office's alert – the GAO Daybook : *http://www.gao.gov/faq/faq.htm#2.2* provides information on released (or soon-to-be released GAO reports, testimony, letters or hearings). If an item has been released, there often will be a hypertext link to the report directly from the e-mail message.
- **Census:** The Census Bureau *http://www.census.gov/mp/www/subscribe.html* has four mailing lists. Reporters and editors may be

SOURCES

ONLINE RESOURCES/ARTICLES:

"Improve newsgroup reading with search engines" by Tracy Swedlow. IDGnet, Jan. 15, 1998: *http://www.idg.net/idg_frames/english/content.cgi?vc=docid_0-76317.html*

most interested in the *I-Net* Bulletin that lists new data files, reports and features of the Census site as well as the press release list that alerts the media about significant statistics in Census Bureau reports and data files.

- **Education:** If education is your beat, access the alert put out by the Department of Education two or three times a week: *http://www.ed.gov/MailingLists/*
- **Environment:** The Environmental Protection Agency (EPA) has a number of discussion lists that are particularly useful for those who cover environmental issues. To access the lists go to *http://www.epa.gov/epahome/listserv.htm* You can subscribe to alerts that deal with everything from press releases to Federal Register notices dealing with the environment. Of particular interest to journalists would be Internet news briefs, a list that feeds you a weekly selection of environmental Internet sites or a daily current awareness list called OPPT-Newsbreak.
- **Foreign Affairs:** The Secretary of States' office: *http://www.state.gov/www/listservs.html* offers a number of discussion lists that alert reporters to developments abroad. The SOS recently started a Kosovo list where you receive, in your e-mail, all press information, situation reports and other remarks on the Kosovo crisis. The SOS also releases over e-mail the Secretary's addresses before Congress, press briefings and background notes on particular countries.

Be sure to check out your state's government Web sites for valuable alert services.

Business

- **IRS:** The IRS Daily Dispatch: *http://www.irs.ustreas.gov/help/newmail/maillist.html* Provides information on tax dates, new additions to the IRS Web site as well as IRS announcements and press releases.
- **Stock Market:** Stocks@Close: *http://www.nsiweb.com/stocks/* Provides an avenue for receiving a nightly Stock Market report. Sent minutes after the close of the trading day, Stocks@Close provides closing prices and daily statistics.
- **Experts:** Business reporters who are looking for experts on important business stories should take advantage of the alerts provided by Profnet: *http://www.profnet.com*. Profnet briefs on business and technology issues are set up to alert reporters to experts on breaking and emerging news. The brief will contain a short synopsis of issues, like "starting salary climbs for new college graduates." A contact will be listed with a phone number and e-mail address.

Health

- **Health statistics:** The Center for Disease Control's Morbidity and Mortality Weekly Report (MMWR) *http://www.cdc.gov/epo/mmwr/mmwr.html* is available via e-mail.
  - The HIV/AIDS Surveillance report *http://www.cdc.gov/nchstp/hiv_aids/stats/hasrlink.htm* is also available in an alert format.
- **Alerts:** The Profnet brief alerts; *http://www.profnet.com* available for business and technology issues are also available for health issues.

Law

- **Supreme Court:** Cornell University Law School's Legal Information Institute (LII) provides a syllabi of U.S. Supreme Court decisions with its LII bulletin alert: *http://www.law.cornell.edu/focus/bulletins.html*
- **Criminal Justice:** If you are following criminal or juvenile justice issues, access the alert JUSTINFO provided by the National Criminal Justice Reference Service (NCJRS): *http://www.ncjrs.org/justinfo/* This alert is published twice a month and contains information on NCJRS products as well as important criminal justice resources on the Internet.

News Filters by Topic and Type

These are services which let you customize the topic you'd like alerts on.

Government

- For comprehensive access to e-mail alerts from all sorts of government agencies, look at Capitol Newswire: *http://www.global-villages.com/capitolnewswire/* a service particularly for journalists covering the DC scene. Choose the topics you want to receive press releases on. Topics include crime, education, the deficit, international trade, medicine and more.

Business

- Through the FreeEDGAR Watch List: *http://www.freeedgar.com/Search/WatchList.asp*, reporters can be notified by e-mail when any company on their watch list submits an electronic filing to the Securities and Exchange Commission (SEC).
- IRS: The IRS has also recently started the Local News Net that alerts you to information that is targeted to your geographic area. Just click on the map for the state you want and instructions for how to subscribe to the regional list will appear: *http://www.irs.ustreas.gov/bus_info/tax_pro/where_list/*
- Use PR-Newswire: *http://www.prnmedia.com/prnemail* to stay on top of business news. On PRN, you create a profile that allows you to schedule e-mail delivery times, select the full-text, headline or abstract of press releases, select particular states, industries, subject areas or companies, or use advanced profile to use more specific terms. Press Line *http://www.pressline.de/email-service/index.us.phtml* is a similar tool.

Health

- NewsDesk, a service of PR Newswire: *http://www.newsdesk.com/register.htm* provides a great source for those covering health or technology issues. Journalists can register for free and create user profiles that reflect their beat. NewsDesk carries breaking news releases, company and product background information, case studies, white papers, biographies, photos – and even video clips and radio soundbytes – from many companies. You will receive a daily e-mail with the list of releases that match your profile. Hyperlinks to the appropriate releases are provided.

News story filters:

- **NewsIndex:** *http://newsindex.com/delivered.html* Set up a profile using subject keywords and have news stories from over 250 news sources around the world delivered to your e-mail. Stories that appear to match your keywords are delivered to you daily.

- **Quickbrowse:** *http://www.quickbrowse.com.* As its title suggests, the service is meant to provide an easy and quick way of browsing the Net. A journalist who wanted to view the sites of all major US papers on a daily basis developed this site. Through Quickbrowse, one can combine multiple sites (say the feature sections of 5 newspapers) and then have those sites delivered to your e-mail at a particular time.

Monitor Web site changes:

- **Informant:** *http://informant.dartmouth.edu/* Saves search engine queries and Web sites (like a company or court's page), checks them periodically, and sends you e-mail whenever there are new or updated Web pages. The Informant searches Alta Vista, Excite, Lycos and Infoseek.

- **TracerLock:** *http://peacefire.org/tracerlock* Monitors search engines for you and notifies you by e-mail when a new instance of a search term is found.

- **NetMind:** *http://mindit.netmind.com* This service monitors Web sites you have designated and allows you to detail the information you are tracking. You can track a full page, paragraph or text, images, links, or keywords. This tracking capability can be used to monitor particular numbers (like prices, sales projections, trading volume, etc.) and for automatic notification when any of those numbers cross a certain threshold that you specify. You can be notified by e-mail or on the Web.

Newsgroup message filters:

- **Deja:** *http://www.deja.com* DejaNews has renamed itself "Deja." Register for the My Deja service to set up message filters using Deja Tracker. Once you set up a filter you can do a regular Deja search for messages and then click on "Track this search for me" and subsequent messages which match that search will be saved for you.

- **NewsSieve:** *http://jod.informatik.uni-bonn.de:8080/eng/* A service from Germany, this service filters Usenet (newsgroup) messages for you.

- Find information about other filtering services at Information Filtering Resources: *http://www.ece.umd.edu/medlab/filter/*

Exercises

- Sign up for My Deja: *http://www.deja.com* and set up a tracker on messages about a topic you are interested in.
- Sign up for one of the alert services mentioned above or find one from a state or local government agency.
- Sign up for Informant: *http://informant.dartmouth.edu* and set it to save a search for a topic of interest.

World Wide Web

The last edition of *A Guide to Computer Assisted Research* had a scant few pages dedicated to the World Wide Web. This edition could be called *A Guide to Using the World Wide Web for Research*. So many of the previous means by which the documents and information found in Internet connected computers were located and retrieved (telnet, ftp, gopher) have been wrapped into the World Wide Web. Elements of some other Internet functions (e-mail, forums, chat) have been wrapped into Web sites. The software needed to use the Web has wrapped in the software required to do those, now almost obsolete, functions. The Web has become an almost interchangeable word with the Internet – when people say they looked on the Internet, they mean the Web. But, in fact, the Web is only one of the functions of the Internet. Here's how it differs from the other Internet tools.

- **Multi-media:** WWW pages, through the use of html (hyper-text markup language) coding, can incorporate text, images, sound files and video clips all together. With ftp and gopher you could retrieve only single-element files (a text file, sound file or photo file). The ability to deliver multiple mediums in a single package has created a greater flexibility in information packaging and delivery.
- **Interactive:** Whereas you couldn't respond or comment to a gopher document, you can click on a highlighted link on a Web page and get an e-mail box for sending an immediate message to the compiler of the site. This instant access to the "publisher" allows easier connection to the creator of the pages' content (always a frustration with gopher documents).
- **Hyperlinked:** Gopher documents stood alone. Web pages use "hypertext" links to connect you to other pages in the Web site or to other pages on different Web sites. This ability to go deeper into a Web site and to connect information on other Web sites has created a 3-dimensional information space. The two-dimensional physical characters of a page (length and width) are joined by a third dimension, depth.

Web pages use hypertext transfer protocol (http) to deliver the information. When you see "http" you know you'll be retrieving a Web page.

Use of the World Wide Web in Reporting and Research

Web sites are the bread-and-butter of online research. Documents from government sites provide background material and verification. Reports on association sites lead to story ideas and help you find experts and authorities.

Libraries of online books help with ready reference questions and routine fact look-up. News site articles help with current events and help you gauge how others have covered stories. See the sections on individual types of content sites on the Web for more ideas for using these resources in reporting and research.

WWW Anecdote

Ask any journalist or researcher who has used the Web to tell a favorite story about how something they found on the Web saved the day. I guarantee they'll have one.

SOURCES

BOOKS:

The Complete Beginner's Guide to the World Wide Web, by Scott Western. Take That, 1998.

A Journalist's Guide to the Internet: The Net as a Reporting Tool, by Christopher Callahan. Allyn & Bacon, 1999.

The Electronic Journalist: Using the Internet and other electronic resources, by Randy Reddick and Elliot King. HBJ College and School Division, 1997 (new edition coming soon).

But here is one of my favorites, from Gina Fann, a reporter formerly at the *Tennessean:*

While reporting on the Peterbilt-UAW local strike, I was tipped at 5:35 PM CST Wednesday that the National Labor Relations Board had ruled in the union's favor on a series of unfair labor practice charges. The Local NLRB office closes and disappears at 4:30 PM; I had no names of sources there to call at home, so no way to confirm with 6 PM deadline looming. The Union quickly sent out a press release celebrating its "win" over the company; the company quickly sent out a press release saying only that NLRB had set a hearing date on complaint.

With conflicting reports on an issue that would ultimately become one paragraph of the overall six-month strike story (and not feeling up to speed on labor because I've been off that beat more than a year), I turned to the 'net for help. Checked http://www.nlrb.gov, knowing it would probably have some procedural steps to eyeball AND would be reliable because of the .gov. Clicked on the "facts" link in the home page. Sure enough, the fourth item, "How Are Unfair Labor Practice Cases Processed?", outlined what I needed, showing there was no way the NLRB would have skipped its own due process regulations and ruled in *anyone's* favor without first having a hearing. With my editor pressing, I had to report simply that "the National Labor Relations Board may set a January hearing to address the union's unfair labor practices complaint ..." because I couldn't confirm anything more.

The next morning, I called the NLRB again after 8 a.m. The Nashville Resident Officer confirmed, rather strongly, that the NLRB indeed had NOT ruled on the charges, in EITHER side's favor, but hoped to either announce a settlement or file a possible complaint against the company sometime in the next week. If the latter were the case, they'd try to get a hearing date, probably in January. That gave me a quick response when irate union members called and e-mailed me and my editor today, insisting that our facts were wrong and we had been the "victims of a misinformation campaign" and should run a correction. Nope. We weren't wrong. We could've been, though, if we hadn't had some fast, reliable way to at least verify NLRB procedures.

What you need to use the World Wide Web

You must have full Internet access through an Internet provider service or a direct line into your network to be able to use the WWW.

You also need "browser" software. This software translates the hypertext mark-up language (html) used to create Web pages and displays it on your computer screen in a readable, usable way.

The first Web browser was Mosaic, developed by Marc Andreessen who went on to found Netscape. Since then there have been hundreds of different browsers developed but Netscape's Navigator and Microsoft's Internet Explorer are fighting it out as the main browsers used. (See a list of browser software and the types of operating systems they best work on at BrowserWatch: *http://browserwatch.internet.com/browsers.html*)

No matter which browser software you use, they all have the same sorts of functions. I'll specify the ways you would use Internet Explorer (IE) and Netscape Navigator (N) to perform the following functions.

WHERE DO YOU WANT TO GO TODAY?
Putting in the Web address

This is where you type in the Web address (also known as the URL: uniform resource locator). The Web address starts with *http://* – this indicates what type of protocol to use, in this case a hyper-text transfer protocol for retrieving a Web page. The second part of the address is the domain name that identifies which computer on the Internet network you want to go to. The domain name (also known as the IP – Internet Protocol – address) is the translation of the numerical IP address into a more easily remembered name.

- **IE:** type the address into the **ADDRESS** box in the top bar of the browser OR under **FILE**, select **OPEN** and type in the address
- **N:** type the address into the **LOCATION** box in the top bar of the browser OR under **FILE**, select **OPEN PAGE** and type in the address
- Hit the *enter* key
- *Tip: CASE MATTERS, use the correct upper and lower case. There are no spaces in a Web address.*
- *Tip: Recent versions of both browsers have http:// as the default so if you are finding a Web address you don't need to type in the "http://" part*
- *Tip: If you are using Navigator and you are going to a Web site that has "www" as the prefix and "com" as the suffix, all you have to type in is the middle part.*
- *Tip: Browsers are getting smart – they remember the address of Web sites you have recently used so if you start to type in an address it will fill out the rest of it for you automatically.*

Exercise: connect to Yahoo: http://www.yahoo.com, then go to the Poynter Institute (www.poynter.org).

SCROLLING THROUGH CYBERSPACE:
Moving through Web sites

- Scrolling on a Web page:

    IE and N: Scroll up and down the page with the margin arrows. On the right side will be arrows that let you go up and down, at the bottom there might be horizontal arrows if the Web page you are displaying is wider than the screen.

- Moving through the Web site:

    IE and N: Click on hypertext links – underlined links, often in blue, by clicking on the left mouse button. You can tell something is a hypertext link when the cursor arrow changes to a hand with a pointing finger. These links might take you out of the Web site you are in and connect you to another Web site. You can tell where you are going by looking at the status bar at the bottom of the Web browser. It will show you the address of the Web page you are going to and will show you the download status. When you get "Document Done" in the status bar you know the download has been completed.

- Navigation buttons on the page can be used to get you around to different sections of the Web site. There is often a "homepage" link to get you back to the front page of the Web site.

Exercise: Go to the U.S. Census Bureau Web site: http://www.census.gov and click on some of the hypertext links

GET BACK TO WHERE YOU ONCE WERE:
Following the trail of crumbs

- **IE and N:** Use the *back* and *forward* buttons to move back and forth one page at a time through pages you've already gone to.
- **IE and N:** Use the *Go* button on the toolbar. Click on GO and get a list of pages you've been to, select one to jump directly to that page.
- *Tip: The pages you go back to have been cached in the browser – you are actually getting a saved copy of the page you went to, you are not going back to the Web site and re-retrieving the page. If you are going back to a page that is frequently updated you might want to **Reload** (see instructions below).*

Exercise: Get back to the Poynter homepage by using one of these techniques.

YOU CAN GO HOME AGAIN: Getting home/setting home

Set your browser to go directly to the Web site you use most frequently or that you would like to have as the one it goes to when you open up your browser. This could be a favorite news site, your organization's homepage, an often-used search site. Then, when you hit the **HOME** button you will go directly to that site.

This function is not only done differently in the two different browsers but also on different versions of the same browser. Here is how they are done in the latest versions of IE (4.0) and Netscape Navigator (4.04).

- **IE:** Click **VIEW** on the toolbar – select **INTERNET OPTIONS** – click the **GENERAL** tab. Put in the box the address of the site you want to have as your "home" site.
- **N:** Click **EDIT** and select **PREFERENCES** – click on **Navigator** – in the Home Page section put in the address you want as your default Web site.

Exercise: Change the default address to CNN: http://www.cnn.com

STUCK? Reload

If the download you are doing stops in the middle or if you are at a Web site where the page is frequently updated you can have the Web page you are requesting re-sent.

- **IE:** Click the **REFRESH** button
- **N:** Click the **RELOAD** button

LOVE THAT SITE? WANT TO FIND IT AGAIN?
Save the address

- **IE:** Click **FAVORITES** on the toolbar and select **ADD TO FAVORITES.** The address will go to the bottom of the list.
- **N:** Click **BOOKMARKS** and select **ADD BOOKMARK.**
- *Tip: In Navigator, use FILE BOOKMARK (instead of ADD) to put the bookmark into a particular folder you've set up.*
- *Tip: Both Navigator and Explorer let you organize your bookmarks. Click on the Help file and go to Favorite Web sites – organizing in folder (for IE) or Bookmarks, editing (for N) for more information about how to manage your addresses.*

Exercise: Go to Deja: http:www.deja.com and add it to your address list.

WHERE'S THAT WORD I SEARCHED FOR?

If your search leads you to a long document or a complicated Web page you can find where the word you are looking for is on the page.

- **IE:** Click **EDIT** on the toolbar, highlight **Find on this page,** fill in the box with the word you want to locate and hit find
- **N:** Click **EDIT,** highlight **Find in page**, fill in the box with the word you want to locate and hit find

Exercise: Go to a copy of the Emancipation Proclamation, http://www. nara.gov/exhall/featured-document/eman/emanproc.html – see if it says "slavery" anywhere.

NEVER MIND

If you've started to load a page and it's taking too long or you decide you didn't really want to go there, click the **STOP** button.

PAPER, PLEASE: The print function

- **IE and N:** Click the **Print** button OR click **File** on the toolbar, highlight **Print** OR hit **CTRL P**

OTHER BROWSER FUNCTIONS

- Want to see when a **Web page was last updated**?

   IE: Under **FILE**, click **Properties**, look at **Created** And **Modified** dates.

   N: Under **VIEW**, click **Page Info**, look at **Last Modified**
- Need a bit **bigger or smaller font** on the page?

   IE: Under **VIEW**, click **Fonts** - Increase or decrease the size

   N: Under **VIEW**, click **Increase Font** or **Decrease Font**
- Want to see what the **HTML** (hypertext transfer markup language) code looks like for the page?

   IE: Under **VIEW,** click **Source**

   N: Under **VIEW,** click **Page Source**

If you can do these functions, you can get around in the World Wide Web.

LOOKING AT WEB SITES

Web sites are sponsored by different types of groups – associations, educational institutions, commercial sites and companies, government organizations and agencies, and individuals (see the next section for details about the sponsors of Web sites). The design and arrangement of each site is different and you must explore to see the features and functions available in each site. In general, however, most Web sites have some or all of the following:

- **Search function:** A way to find pages or items within the Web site
- **Features and sections:** Lists or buttons linking to special areas of the site
- **Help files:** Information about how to use the site effectively
- **Site map:** A graphical map or index of the Web site's features. Not all sites have them, but they should
- **About this site:** Information about who put this site together and why
- **User mail/comment:** Interactive feature

Some also have chat groups, alert services or other types of functions.

Exercise

Go to APB Online: *http://www.apbonline.com*, a Web site for police and crime news. Look for the following functions and features.

- **Search:** Find the search feature and look for items which contain the word "busted".
- **Features list:** Where can you find information on missing children?
- **Help:** Locate where there is information about how to use the site.
- **About this site:** What is the mission statement of the site? Who sponsors APB?
- **User mail/comment:** How can people send mail to APB?
- **Currency of the information:** Can you find the date the material was posted?
- **Alert service:** Is there any way to get automatic updates and news releases from the site?

With all Web sites you need to take some time to look over the layout of the site, locate specific features and functions and get to know the contents of the site.

Tips and Traps when using the World Wide Web

- **Know the site creator:** All things look equal on the Web. Be careful in determining who is sponsoring and contributing information to the site you are looking at. Do some background research before you use their information as background research! See more tips in "Evaluating Information Online" (139-142).
- **Traffic can get heavy:** Even with a fast line and reliable connection to the Internet, Web traffic can get heavy, especially to popular sites. Don't rely on a Web site to be available when needed.
- **Don't get lost:** Went to a great site last week and you just know it will have the information you need? Can't find it again? You didn't use your bookmark! Learn how to use the bookmark feature of your Web browser, be consistent in it's use and clean it up every so often. (Bookmark editing will let you annotate what information is available on the site or what story you used information from the site for – time taken now will save time later, guaranteed.)
- **Data is dirty** (on paper, electronically, over the phone...): Use healthy skepticism (and a second source) if you are going to use information you found online (or, for that matter, in a book or magazine or from a person). Consider the source of the information – data from a government source might be more reliable than data provided in the press release from a special interest group. If the information you are going to use is critical to your story, or the key point you are making, take the time to verify the information from another source.
- **Cite Sites:** How do you cite the source of information you get? Does the medium used to retrieve the information from an agency matter, or is it just the source of the information you need to attribute? Figure out citation guidelines for your newsroom. Here are some sites about citing Internet sources:
  - A Brief Citation Guide for Internet Sources in History and the Humanities, by Melvin E. Page: *http://www.fordham.edu/halsall/cite.html*
  - Columbia Guide to Online Style: *http://www.columbia.edu/cu/cup/cgos/idx_basic.html*

WWW Contents

Think of the World Wide Web as a big circle. Slice the circle into three parts. These three slices represent the contents of the World Wide Web.

One part contains Web sites with valuable, useful, credible information.

One part contains Web sites that help you locate Web sites with information.

The final part is trash, porno, propaganda, and personal pages about people's pets. (Unfortunately, this might be the biggest slice of the three).

As a journalist or researcher using the Web, you'll want to concentrate on the first two parts and figure out how to recognize and avoid the last part. This section will describe the valuable information content Web sites, where they come from, how to use them. The next section will go into the different kinds of searching Web sites that help you find these content sites. In the section on Evaluating Information Online you'll get some tips on how to avoid the last part.

How to recognize Web content sites

The most important clue in recognizing Web sites with content and information is to look at the "top level domain" (TLD) indicated at the suffix of the Web address. They will give you clues about the source of the Web site. Knowing these and knowing how to use them in searching for Web sites will help make your Web use more efficient.

There are currently seven TLDs that indicate different kinds of domains used primarily for U.S.-based Web sites. The UK and some other countries use slight variations of these domains. There is also a list of country codes used as the suffix to indicate country of origin (you can find the list of country domains at *http://www.theodora.com/country_digraphs.html*). The current domain types are:

.gov – Government sites

.com – Commercial sites – businesses (UK and others use .co)

.org – Organization sites – associations

.edu – Educational sites – schools (UK and others use .ac)

.mil – Military sites

.net – Networks

.int – Organizations established by international treaties

There has been such growth on the Web that the current name registration is becoming overwhelmed. Relevant names for a company might already be used by another company. The naming needs to expand. The following are new Top Level Domains that have been proposed:

store – merchants

web – parties emphasizing Web activities

arts – arts and cultural-oriented entities

rec – recreation/entertainment sources

info – information services

nom – individuals

SOURCES

DOMAIN NAME FAQ:

http://www.networksolutions.com/ help/registration/index.html Great overview of the whole registration process.

The International Internet Address and Domain Name System by Robert Fashler. *http://www.davis.ca/topart/ domainam.htm* Provides good background on the domain name system.

There are some other Web address conventions that can be helpful in identifying Web sites: They are not consistently used, but worth a try:

State government sites: http://www.state.**.us

** stands for the two-letter state code – like the one used by the Postal Service – find state abbreviations on the U.S. Postal Service site at: *http://www.usps.gov/ncsc/lookups/usps_abbreviations.htm#states*

State-level government agencies: http://www.***.state.**.us

*** stands for the agency acronym, the ** is the state abbreviation.

County government sites: http://www.co.******.**.us

****** stands for the county name or abbreviated name, the ** is the state abbreviation.

City government sites: http://www.ci.*****.**.us

***** is the city name, ** is the state abbreviation

Read More:

Top-Level Domains: *http://www.dns.net/dnsrd/tld.html*

Who publishes Web sites with content

The domain names give broad categories of the sponsors of Web sites with content, but it needs to be broken down a bit more. Following are the types of sponsors of Web sites with content of value to journalists and researchers. In the section that follows we'll look at each type, what kind of information they provide and why, what journalists can make of those sites, tips and traps in using the sites and some ways to locate those types of sites.

- Government agencies
- Organizations and associations
- Commercial enterprises/businesses
- Educational institutions
- Libraries
- Military
- News organizations/publications
- Individuals

GOVERNMENT AGENCIES

Government agencies were some of the earliest users of the Web and now most government agencies and branches, from local city government up to national governmental departments around the world, have some level of representation on the Web.

According to the Jan. 1999 Internet Domain Survey: *http://www.nw.com/zone/WWW/dist-byname.html* there are 651,200 hosts on the Internet using the top-level domain .gov.

Government Web sites can be identified by the .gov at the end of the Web address. (See above for the Web address structure for state and local government agencies.)

Types of information they provide

Reports, statistics, texts of speeches, documents, personnel directories and biographical information, forms and information about the structure and activities of the agency.

Why they provide it

Government is in the business of information distribution. It is part of its responsibility. It needs to inform citizens about the activities of its agencies and provide ways to get involved. Government Web sites are an economical way to provide access to the information agencies have compiled.

Uses in reporting and research

- Go to interviews with background and facts that your source may not want to tell you.
- Provide a reality check for information gleaned from interviews or other reports. Read texts of speeches, find voting records when covering legislators to see if their statements and votes match current statements.
- Find experts in agencies through directories.
- Find statistics that help illustrate a point you are trying to make or put an event into a broader context.
- Get alerts and news releases from agencies.
- Get information from the agency after office hours or when no one is available.

Tips and traps

- Information found on government sites is as reliable and credible as it would be distributed by any other medium. If you would use the agency as a source, you can trust the information found on its Web site.
- Information on government Web sites usually does not pre-date the Web – about 1995. If you want older information you'll need to contact the agency.
- Government agencies often distribute the latest information and reports via the Web site, but not always. Locating a report on the Web should be followed up with a call to the agency to see if there is new information not yet released. The Web does not automatically make data more current if the agency hasn't released new information; don't get frustrated that the most current report on a topic cites 1995 data – government moves slowly.
- There is no consistent way of organizing information used on government sites. You will have to look over the sections and features carefully to get a sense of the types and arrangements of information.
- Your first stop when learning the Web should be to your local and state government sites so you can learn what information is readily available to you.

Examples and Exercises for Government sites

- You are a business reporter and hear that the largest employer in your town is going to be laying off 1/3 of the employees. You need to background the company's financial status. Find the latest 10-K filings for a large public company in your area. Use the EDGAR (Electronic Data Gathering, Analysis, and Retrieval) database from the Securities and Exchange Commission: *http://www.sec.gov* (click on EDGAR Database)
- In a story on an "English-only" referendum being proposed, you want to add information about the demographics of your county, par-

ticularly the Hispanic population. Search for population statistics for your county in the Census Bureau Web site: *http://www.census.gov*

- You're doing a story on Medicare reform and want to include quotes by the President on the topic. Look for mentions of "medicare" in the President's speeches and addresses at the White House site: *http://www.whitehouse.gov* (click on The Virtual Library).

- A large group of refugees from Kosovo have been sent to your town. In covering the story, you want to know what sort of federal assistance has been proposed. Check the status of the Kosovar Albanian Refugee Humanitarian Assistance Act of 1999 in Thomas – the Federal Legislative Web site at *http://thomas.loc.gov*

- You are the education writer and the new Superintendent of Schools is from Bahrain, you want to do some research on his educational background in Bahrain. Find out about the educational system in Bahrain from the Ministry of Education: *http://www.education.gov.bh/*

- A child in Florida has been killed by his mother's boyfriend. A cop on the case said, "Well, of course, that is what it usually is – kids aren't killed by a parent but by a friend of the parent." Verify the accuracy of his statement by checking the Florida Department of Children and Families Web site at *http://www.state.fl.us/cf_web/*

Finding government sites

- Guess. Use your knowledge of Web addressing for government sites to guess what the address might be for a particular agency. Where, for example, would you find the Internal Revenue Service?

- U.S. Federal Government Agencies on the Web: *http://www.lib.lsu.edu/gov/fedgov.html*

- State and Local Government on the Net: *http://www.piperinfo.com/state/states.html*

- Governments on the World Wide Web: *http://www.gksoft.com/govt/en/* – more than 12,000 entries from 219 countries

- Political Resources on the Net: *http://www.agora.stm.it/politic/*

Read More

Government Information on the Internet, 2nd Ed., by Greg Notess. Bernan Associates, 1998

Government on the Net, by James Evans. Nolo Press, 1998.

How to Access the Federal Government on the Internet 1998, by Bruce Maxwell. Congressional Quarterly, 1997.

ORGANIZATIONS AND ASSOCIATIONS

Every issue, philosophy, physical disease, occupation and recreation are represented by some group or another.

Over 744,200 Web addresses on the Web point to organization sites.

You can recognize organization sites from the .org at the end of the address.

- These are promotional sites, they want to put the best spin on their company and their activities – remember that when looking at the information. No one is monitoring their site for credibility or for false claims.
- Annual reports on corporate sites are frequently in Adobe Acrobat format (PDF). You'll need to download the Acrobat reader to be able to view those documents (see chapter on Downloading and Re-using Information on Web sites).

Examples and exercises for business sites

- The mid-section emergency exit door of a USAir MD 80 blows out. What rows of the airplane were nearest the door? Look for the seating charts on the USAir site: *http://www.usair.com*
- There's a rumor that the new head of your town's United Way effort is James Postl, who had been the president of Nabisco. You're doing a background check on him. What did the company have to say about Postl's leaving? (figure out the address....)

  (Extra points if you can go figure out where Postl is now.)
- You're a health and nutrition columnist and are doing a column on the fat content of fast foods. Check out the nutrition information on the Burger King, McDonald's, and Wendy's sites. (Find the Web addresses, and remember, there are no punctuation marks in addresses.)

Finding business sites

- BizWeb: *http://www.bizweb.com*: links to over 43,000 businesses listed by category
- Annual Reports Gallery: *http://www.reportgallery.com/* Links to the pages within corporate sites which contain the annual report
- How to find a company's annual report online: *http://www.zpub.com/sf/arl/arl-how.html*

EDUCATIONAL INSTITUTIONS

The Internet was originally the domain of education. You had to be affiliated with a university or college or think tank to tap into the network of networks. Now, educational institutions – from kindergarten to graduate school – are using the Web not just to communicate with each other, but to promote themselves and share information.

There are over 5,000,000 .edu addresses according to the Jan. 1999 survey of top domain names.

Educational sites can be identified by the .edu in the address. Some non-U.S. educational sites use .ac instead of .edu.

Types of information they provide

Information about departments and courses available, faculty biographies and contact information and student directories. Information about admissions, administration. Faculty and student publications and projects. Course syllabi. Some have "virtual tours" of the facilities.

Why they provide it

They want to attract students and provide promotional information. They want to share studies and research done by faculty. They use the Web as the new media lab for teaching students about Web design and usage.

Uses in reporting and research

- Locate experts through faculty directories or course descriptions.
- Get information about the school when covering events that might have happened there.
- Find research reports.

Tips and traps

- These are essentially promotional sites, you won't find anything negative about the college or school there.
- Some school sites contain no more than a brochure about the school would, others have rich and vast resources available. None of them contain all the material generated by the school, so use these as starting points, not definitive collections.
- Some elementary, middle and high school sites were taken on as student projects and have not been maintained. Be sure to check the date of the last updates to the page.

Examples and exercises for education sites

- A source tells you that someone named Brownsberger at the Harvard Division on Addictions is a great source to talk to about drug law enforcement. Find him.
- You've been asked by the local university to teach a class on using the Web for research and writing on the Web for journalism students. Look at some syllabi done by others teaching similar courses: World Lecture Hall: *http://www.utexas.edu/world/lecture/*
- You're the education reporter in St. Petersburg, Florida. It's the weekend and you hear a rumor that students at Northeast High are going to stage a huge protest on Monday because of new, restrictive dress codes that will be enforced. You need to talk to someone in the administration. What do you do?

Finding education sites

- All About College: *http://www.allaboutcollege.com* Links to colleges and universities by state and country.
- UniGuide Guide to U.S. Universities: *http://www.aldea.com/guides/gu/attframes3.html* Get all kinds of contact information and links.
- Web66: International School Web Site Registry: *http://web66.coled.umn.edu/schools.html* Links to kindergarten through high school Web sites, by state and country.

LIBRARIES

Libraries are found in universities, schools, and associations. There are national, state, and local libraries. There are legal, medical, business libraries. Though they are usually found within the sites of the sponsoring organization, some (like the Library of Congress) stand alone. Some don't even exist outside the Web, like the Internet Public Library:

http://www.ipl.org. Library sites fill the mission of the library itself, to collect, organize, and facilitate the use of information.

Many public libraries in the US use the Web address structure of: http://www.lib.ci.****.**.us: **** is the city name, ** is the two-letter state code or www.*****.lib.**.us: **** is the city or county name, ** is the two-letter state code.

Types of information they provide

Online catalogs of the library collection. Many have guides for how to use the Internet. Special resource guides. Access to databases. Local libraries will have area specific information and resources.

Why they provide it

Libraries live to organize and share information, Web sites are designed to do that.

Uses in reporting and research

- Find local and regional information in public library sites.
- Find experts by locating authors of books on a topic in online catalogs.
- Find librarians working in specialty libraries and use them as a resource for questions on a topic.

Tips and traps

- Some library sites are just informational sites about the library. Others are full of information and have to really be browsed through. Take the time to get to know your local library resources.
- Some of the services available on public library sites can only be used by library cardholders.

Examples and exercises for library sites

- Use one of the library finders listed below and locate a Web site for a library in your vicinity. Look the site over – what did you find that you didn't expect to find?
- Find literacy programs in the Dallas area using the Dallas Public Library Community Information Database: *http://www.lib.ci.dallas.tx.us/*
- You want to find a listing of all the mayors of Minneapolis over the years. Check the Minnesota Public Library: *http://www.hennepin.lib.mn.us/* Fugitive Fact File (found in the Reference Tools section).

Finding library sites

- SJCPL's List of Public Libraries with WWW Services: *http://www.sjcpl.lib.in.us/Databases/PubLibServFind.html*
- School Libraries on the Web: A Directory: *http://www.voicenet.com/~bertland/libs.html*
- State Library Web Sites: *http://www.dpi.state.wi.us/dlcl/pld/statelib.html*
- LibWeb: *http://sunsite.Berkeley.EDU/Libweb/* Over 2700 library Web pages from libraries in over 70 countries, there is a searchable database to find libraries by type or location.

Read More

Library of Congress Online, by Robert S. Want. Want Publications, 1999.

MILITARY

I was surprised when I saw there were over 1,500,000 pages on the Web with .mil in the address (according to the 1999 survey of top level domains). But then I saw there were over 600 official sites for the U.S. Navy alone. For the Army there are separate sites for bases and units. I can see now how that can add up.

Types of information they provide

Statistics and specification on equipment and personnel. Background on military bases. History of military units.

Why they provide it

These are promotional sites and also used as ways to get information and give support to active personnel and veterans.

Uses in reporting and research

- Get background on different military units
- Find statistics and background on weapons
- Find contacts at different bases to talk to

Tips and traps

- Be sure you are looking at an official site. There are lots of military enthusiasts and veterans who create official looking Web pages that aren't officially sanctioned. A good clue is official sites will have .mil in the address.
- Don't expect military secrets or internal information to appear on the Web site. These are distribution mechanisms for what the military wants you to know.

Exercises and examples for military sites

- A Harrier GR7 from the U.K. Royal Air Force crashed into the crowd during an air show demonstration. You need background on the plane. Get a profile from the RAF Web site at *http://www.raf.mod.uk/*
- A source tells you he was at the Army's Aberdeen Proving Ground for five years where he learned all about chemical warfare. Could he have learned about chemical warfare there and how can you verify he was there? *http://www.apg.army.mil/*
- There is an explosion at the U.S. Coast Guard Base in Cape Cod, Massachusetts. Use these two sources to find information about the base: *http://www.uscg.mil/units.html* and *http://www.militarycity. com/moves/baseguid.htm* Which one was easier to use? Which had the more reliable information?

Finding Military Sites

- Military Data Resource: *http://www.militarydataresource.com/* Organized by U.S., Worldwide, Weapon Systems, Weapon Builders, etc. – over 2,500 links.
- Rongstad's Worldwide Military Links *http://members.aol.com/ rhrongstad/private/milinksr.htm* An impressive personal effort to compile military links by country, branch, and other categories (including a new one on Prisoners of War).

- Ultimate Collection of News Links: *http://pppp.net/links/news/*
- The MIT List of Radio Stations on the Internet: *http://wmbr.mit.edu/stations/list.html* Listing over 8,000 radio stations around the world.
- PubList.Com: *http://www.publist.com/* Information about 150,000 publications including Web address if there is one.
- Ultimate TV: *http://www.ultimateTV.com*
- E-Zine List: *http://www.meer.net/~johnl/e-zine-list/* Information on more than 3,700 e-zines.
- Current Awareness Resources using Internet Audio and Video: *http://gwis2.circ.gwu.edu/~gprice/audio.htm* One of several great resources compiled by Gary Price from George Washington University.

INDIVIDUALS

Anyone can register for a Web domain, and they do. The number of Web sites that lets people create their own Web pages is growing and so, too, is the number of individuals taking advantage of these services. Today anyone can be a publisher. Individuals' hobbies, philosophies, obsessions, and experiences are all out there on the Web. Much of the third slice of the Web, the trash, porno, mis-information, and just plain drivel come from individuals. But there are also some very useful resources compiled by individuals. It takes some looking and a lot of evaluation once you find them.

You can often recognize personal/individual's pages by the tilda (~) in the address (i.e., *http://www.geocities.com/~*) On GeoCities alone over 3 million people have created personal pages. There are hundreds of places offering space for people who want to create their own sites.

Types of information they provide

Information about stars, singers, athletes. Compilations of links on strange and interesting topics. Stories about personal experiences. Products they want to sell. Background on hobbies or collections. Personal biographies (complete with pictures of the family and pets) and family genealogies. The range of interests and topics that individuals write about covers everything under the sun.

Why they provide it

The Web has become the ultimate vanity press. This is a way for people to "share" their life's interest, their obsessions. What in the past might have been a newsletter sent to a few people is now a Web site available to the world. Some are inspired by philanthropic instinct, they feel the information they have is important to share. Some really do just seem to have too much time on their hands. This is the best and the worst of the Web, anyone can publish anything and ANYONE can publish ANYTHING.

Uses in reporting and research

- Looking for the off-beat? Want to find the fringe? Individual pages can help.
- Personal pages are becoming so common, checking to see if someone you are covering has created a page should be part of your backgrounding routine (one of the students in the Columbine High

School massacre, Eric Harris, had a personal page on AOL [America Online]).

- Looking for people with personal experience? Personal Web pages are a great way to locate people who want to share their experiences.

Tips and traps

- Figuring out who put the page together, what their qualifications are, and why they've done it, (key criteria for evaluating Web sites) is often very difficult to do.
- It may look authoritative but it's not necessarily so. No one has checked the material on these pages. Browser beware.
- Compilations and information on individuals' pages may have been a one-time interest but is no longer being kept up to date. Always check when the page was last modified to see how fresh it is.
- Generally information on .edu sites (educational sites) can be considered reliable unless it has a ~ in the address (which indicates this is a personal page sitting on the educational site server). Many universities give space on the computer server to students, and they usually don't monitor the contents.
- Be careful of using "personal pages" (or reading profiles) purported to be by someone who is suddenly the focus of media attention. After the Oklahoma City bombers were named profiles supposedly written by Timothy McVeigh appeared on AOL. Don't get fooled.
- If you go to a personal page on GeoCities or Tripod (found either on the site's directory or from a regular search engine search) it will spawn another window over the one you clicked to. This is actually opening a new browser window and usually contains an ad. You can close the window by clicking on the "x" in the upper right corner of the window.

Examples and exercises for personal pages

- You're doing a feature story on strange collections and hobbies, find collectors of toasters, of subway tokens, and of pogo sticks. Use GeoCities' directory: *http://www.geocities.com/search/*
- You're a photographer and are assigned to shoot a "*pick your favorite band*" concert. Go to some fan sites and find out something about the performances they give, check out some photos.
- Find some personal pages relating to scoliosis. Why might you use these in reporting? Why wouldn't you use them?

Finding personal page

- WhoWhere's Homepage search: *http://homepages.whowhere. lycos.com/* Find pages by a number of different categories. This is the best of the homepage look-up directories.
  (Find a listing of other personal page directories at *http://www. december.com/cmc/info/culture-people-lists.html)*
- The directories on sites which provide personal page services are good places to look. The search function on GeoCities (*http://www.geocities.com*) and Tripod (*http://www.tripod.com*) taps into the interests of hundreds of thousands of people. Find a listing of places offering free personal home pages at *http://www.freeindex. com/webspace/index.html*

- The Web search sites (Go, AltaVista, HotBot, etc.) index personal home pages. A large portion of the items retrieved from a search come from individuals. There are also directories of all kinds of specific types of personal pages (by profession, geographic region, religion). If you are looking for a particular type of person's pages, search for "home page" and the keyword you are looking for.
- Personal Pages Worldwide: College and University Collections: *http://www.utexas.edu/world/personal/* Links to college directories of student home pages on the college's server.
- Yahoo! Personal Home Pages: *http://dir.yahoo.com/Society_ and_Culture/People/Personal_Home_Pages/ Complete_Listing/* More than 60,000 personal pages by name.
- Web rings are made up primarily of personal pages. Find Web rings (see more on Web rings – 99-101) at *http://www.webring.org*

These are just some of the kinds of creators of Web sites. Hospitals, law firms, police agencies, political parties, and churches are some of the other types of organizations which create Web sites. As you explore the Web and encounter Web sites from different types of sponsors, keep in mind who put the Web site together, why they have done it, what kind of information they provide, and how you might use it in your reporting and research. This consciousness about the usefulness of different types of Web sites will serve you well as you start learning how to efficiently and effectively use the Web for research.

SOURCES

BOOKS AND SITES:

The Extreme Searcher's Guide to Web Search Engines, by Randolph Hock. CyberAge Books, 1999.

Search Tools Chart: *http://www. infopeople.org/src/chart.html*

Search Engine Watch: *http://www. searchenginewatch.com* Everything you'd want to know about search engines, thanks to Danny Sullivan.

Web searching: a tutorial on search strategy and syntax: *http://PowerReporting.com/ altavista.html*

WEB SEARCHING BASICS

Remember the big circle we talked about in the previous chapter with three slices that represents the contents of the World Wide Web? One of the slices was for Web sites that help you locate Web sites with content. Commonly referred to as search engines, I prefer to call them search sites because a search engine is simply software which manages the searching of contents of a database and almost every Web site has some kind of search function. Search sites, on the other hand, were created to help Web users locate Web sites. They have a search engine on them, sometimes several, but that is usually only a part of the search site.

We'll go into detail about the different types of search sites on the Web in the next chapter, Web Search Sites. But first we should go over the basics of searching on the Web.

- Focusing the search
- Search engine basics
- Search functions
- Search trouble shooting
- What search sites won't find

Focusing the Search

Look back at the chapter on defining the task and framing the question. Keep these tips on how to focus on the task you need to accomplish and how to be clear about the question you need answered in mind as you start using search sites. They will help you identify the type of search site you should use for specific types of tasks.

Search Engine Basics

All of the search engines on search sites have the same sorts of functions. What differs between the services is how you perform those functions, which are the "default" functions on the site, and where you find the form for conducting the functions.

The first thing you should do when you go to an unfamiliar search site (or even one you've been using, but with some degree of frustration) is to find the search help file. This is sometimes a challenge. The terms they use on different sites for the help file vary and are sometimes not very prominently displayed.

There are three main differences between the search engines used by Web search sites and the traditional archive databases (like Dialog or Nexis):

- **Structured search vs. Natural language:** Dialog and Nexis searches are fairly rigidly constructed; you have to follow the right search syntax. *(car or auto or automotive or automobile) and insurance.*

    Web searches are natural language queries. You can type in the words any way you want, even as a sentence, *"I want to find stuff about automobile insurance."* You can do more structured kinds of searches on Web search sites, but they are designed as natural language search engines.

- **Word match vs. Fuzzy logic:** Traditional database searches retrieve only those documents which match exactly the terms you typed in. Something is either a true match or it is not.

   Web searches use "fuzzy logic", they are not so black or white. They will find exact matches but they'll also retrieve words that are pretty darn close to what you asked for.

- **Chronological display vs. Relevancy ranking:** Traditional database searches rank their results in either chronological or reverse chronological order (oldest to newest or newest to oldest).

   Web searches display results by relevancy, not date. Displayed first will be those pages with the greatest occurrence of the terms you've asked for, or the most prominent location of those terms on the page (in the title or Web address or lead paragraph). The "fuzzy" logic search is why you get so many results in Web site searches, some which don't seem to have the words you've looked for. But the relevancy ranking is why the best material for your search is at the top of the list. Even though you get 245,865 hits on a search, you'll usually find the first 10 or so are the most relevant.

Another thing to be aware of with Web search sites is that some of them actually use the same search engine software. Knowing which software is used can be helpful. If you know the search functions from one search site and another site uses the same search software, then you can be pretty sure how that one will work.

One of the most important things to remember is that when you search the search engine is going to look for the word you typed, not necessarily the word you mean. It's looking for matching characters, not a matching definition. You're looking for Matisse, the artist, but when you type in Matisse you get a software company, a restaurant and other un-related Matisses. You'll want to get specific in your search (put in his first name, too).

Search Functions

Let's look at six basic search functions and how they operate in Web search sites. There are dozens of search services on the Web, for each of the following functions I will profile how some of the major services use these features:

- Boolean logic
- Proximity searching
- Truncation
- Case sensitivity
- Field searching
- Date range searching

For specifics about how each of these operate (or don't operate) in various search sites be sure to read the site's help files. (Also, see the bibliography at the beginning of this chapter for books and Web sites with more detail about Web searching.)

BOOLEAN LOGIC: And, Or, Not

Boolean logic, named for a British mathematician named George Boole (1815-1864), refers, according to Encyclopedia Britannica (*http://www.eb.com*), to the "symbolic system of mathematical logic that represents relationships between entities – either ideas or objects". When used in the context of database searching, it is a way to represent the relationship between search terms.

Web search sites usually have two levels of searching. The level you see on the home page is usually the "simple" search. If you want to take advantage of the more precise searching using Boolean connectors you have to go to the "advanced" search.

One of the problems with many Web search sites is the inability to "nest" search terms. For example, setting up multiple "or" sets, *(money or dollars or moola) and (saving or investing or hoarding)*. The elaborate search relationships you can set-up in the big commercial database services are usually not seen in Web search sites.

There are three logical connectors between search terms: AND, OR, NOT. They are frequently described using a visual representation of the relationship between the terms using overlapping circles, called a Venn diagram.

AND: The AND relationship between search terms would be represented as two overlapping circles. The overlapping part of the circles is the AND set.

You're going to interview the owner of Pampered Pets, a local dog breeder specializing in expensive poodles and you want to prepare by finding some background material. Do an AND search for *poodles (A)* and *breeding (B)*. Retrieved documents would contain BOTH *poodles* AND *breeding* – represented by the C in the Venn diagram below. The AND search is more restrictive than the OR search.

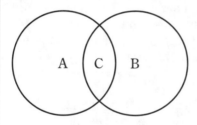

How AND is represented in a few different search sites:

Go, AltaVista – simple search: + *in front of search terms (+poodle +breeding)*

Northern Light and AltaVista – advanced: *type in the whole boolean phrase (poodle AND breeding)*

Go – advanced search: *pull-down box, select "document", "must", contain the "word"*

Yahoo!: *just type in the words, AND is the default search*

Yahoo! – advanced search: *type in search words then click the "Matches on all words" button*

Deja – advanced search: *type in search words then select "all" in the pull-down box*

OR: The OR relationship between search terms would be represented as everything in both of the overlapping circles of the Venn diagram.

You're going a do a big package on health-care financing. You need to find some experts to talk with. Go to the Profnet experts database (*http://www.profnet.com/ped.html*) and do a search on *Medicare (A)* OR *Medicaid (B)*. You'll get entries represented by everything in A, B, and C (with C being documents that have both terms, Medicare and Medicaid, in them.) The OR search is the most inclusive of the logical connectors.

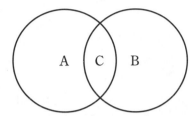

How OR is represented in a few different search sites:

Go, AltaVista – simple search: *just enter terms, the default search is OR*

Go – advanced search: *pull-down box, select "document", "should", contain the "word(s)"*

AltaVista – advanced search: *type in the whole boolean phrase (Medicare OR Medicaid)*

Yahoo! – advanced search only: *type in terms, click on* **"Matches on any words"** *button*

Deja – advanced search: *type in search words then select "any" in the pull-down box*

NOT: NOT is the most dangerous of the Boolean connectors to use. You can inadvertently leave out relevant hits because they happen to contain the word you "NOT" out.

For example, you want to see if there is anything written about a guy named Dave Matthews, but not the Dave Matthews of the Dave Matthews Band. So you search for *"Dave Matthews" (A) NOT band (B)*. The results will be the part represented by the A. The trouble with the search is that it will knock out any articles that said *band* in it including what might have been a great article on Dave Matthews, the guy you are looking for, which happens to say "He played in the high school band…" NOT is usually not a good searching route to take (unless it is to NOT out articles from a particular publication or if it is used in a field search – see below).

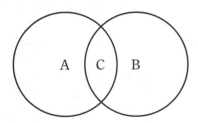

How NOT is represented in a few different search sites:

Go, AltaVista, Yahoo! – simple and advanced search: *put a – in front of the term*

Go – advanced search: *pull-down box, select "document", "should not", contain the "word(s)"*

AltaVista – advanced search: *type in the whole boolean phrase ("dave matthews" AND NOT band)*

Deja – advanced search: there is no NOT function

- **Tip:** Get in the habit of typing boolean connector words in CAPS. Some of the search engine software requires caps, others don't care but to be safe, use CAPS.

Read more:

- Boolean searching on the Internet: *http://www.albany.edu/library/ internet/boolean.html*

PROXIMITY SEARCHING: " "

Proximity is the search function that lets you set the closeness of search terms to each other. If you do a phrase search or have search terms appear near to each other, you are doing a proximity search. In commercial database services, proximity searching can be quite elaborate. You can ask for a word to be within 5 or 10 or 38 words of another word or within the same paragraph. In Web search services, however, there are fewer options.

Of the proximity functions the phrase search is the one that is available on almost every search engine used by Web search sites. It is also the one that is most consistent in how you designate a phrase search in different search engines. Use quotation (" ") marks around the terms you want to search as a phrase.

If you are searching for a phrase, do not forget to use the quotes. If you are covering an art house revival of Salvador Dali's film "Andalusian Dog" and want some background, typing in *andalusian dog* in Go will return 5,483,480 hits (default search when you just type in terms is an OR search).

Typing in +andalusian +dog (an AND search) retrieves 181, which is much better. But typing in "andalusian dog" with the quotation marks will get you 84 hits, virtually all of them relevant.

TRUNCATION: rank ranked ranking ranker ranks

Sometimes you want to search a term by various possible endings or variations of the word. There are two different types:

- **Word endings:** Put in the word stem and truncation symbol and the search will fill in the possible endings. This is a "forward" truncation. Most of the services that have truncation use the asterisk (*) for the truncation symbol. Others do some automatic pluralization (put in a noun and it will automatically look for the plural). Others don't do truncation.
- **Wildcard:** Type in the word with the * in spaces where you want words with any letters in that position to be retrieved. Wildcard searches are useful if you aren't sure how a word is spelled. Is it Johannesburg or Johanesberg or Johanesburg? Search Johan*esb*rg.

TIP: Be conscious when using truncation. If you search for *horse**, you'll get *horse* and *horses* and *horse's,* of course, but you'll also get *horseshoe, horsefly, horseshow, horsehead...* It might be better to just do an OR search and string together the various words you really want searched.

How truncation is done:

AltaVista, HotBot, Northern Light, Yahoo!: *

Go: automatically searches singular and plural

CASE SENSITIVITY: May may

Some of the search engine software will match the case of the word typed in. This is particularly helpful when searching for proper names (especially ones that have a dual meaning). Search for "may" in Go you'll get 47,000,000 plus hits but search for "*May*" and you'll get half as many hits, just proper name May, month of May, or May at the start of a sentence will be retrieved.

Search services with case sensitivity: AltaVista, HotBot, Go

FIELD SEARCHING: title: "how to do field searching"

Field searching may be the most useful way to narrow and focus your search. When you do a field search you are looking for the search term to appear in a particular part of the retrieved page. Different search services offer different types of field searches (check their help files), but here are two of the most useful fields to use in searching:

- **Title:** A title field search will only retrieve pages with your search term in the title of the page. This is useful for broad searches. Relevant documents would probably have in the title the term you are searching for. Looking for background about coal mining? In Go, search "*coal mining*" and get 20,568 hits, but search *title:"coal mining"* and get 266 hits.
  - **AltaVista, Northern Light, and Go:** *title:term*
  - **HotBot:** type the search term you want in the search box, select "the page title" in the pulldown box below the search box.
  - **Yahoo!:** *t:term*
- **Domain or URL:** A Web address (URL) search is a great way to narrow down the search to particular types of sites. If you know that a government agency would be the best, most reliable source for information you are seeking, narrow the search to just *.gov* sites. If you think an association would be the likeliest source, search in the *.org* domain. You need material about fire safety and don't want to get every commercial page selling fire alarms, you just want information from organizations concerned with fire safety. In AltaVista search *domain.org* +*"fire safety"* and get 4,800 hits, *"fire safety"* retrieved 44,000 pages.
  - **AltaVista:** *domain:domain type(org, gov, com, etc.)* or *url:term* (this will look for the term anywhere in the address, i.e., *url:fire* would find *www.fire-quip.com* and *fire.mountlaurel.com/*
  - **Go and Northern Light:** *url:term* (covers domain name or term in the Web address)
  - **Yahoo!:** *u:term*

DATE RANGE SEARCHING

Date searching is one of the staples of commercial database searching. It is a way to get articles from certain time periods or since a certain date. On the Web, date searching is more problematic. It's hard to know if the date being searched is when the information was originally published, when it went onto the Web site, or is just the date of the search site's indexing of that page. In most cases it is the latter, which is actually the least relevant date for researchers.

The way date searching is done on the search sites that provide it is very different, and difficult to describe. It's best to read the help files on the search site you are using to see if date range searching is an option.

SEARCH TROUBLESHOOTING

Too many results: Although the relevancy ranking feature of Web search engine software will probably pull the most relevant results to the top of the list, it is disconcerting to get 14,000,003 hits when you do a search. If this happens, think of ways to narrow it down. Is there a specific domain you'd want to search? Is there a word you can AND into the search to narrow it down?

Too few results: If you get few or no results, check your searching syntax. You may have put a space in where it wasn't needed (in a field search, for example). Check your spelling, you may need to do a wildcard search to get alternate spellings.

Get a good result, but can't get the page: There is often a considerable lag between the times a search site's index is updated. A page which was indexed by a search site might have moved or been deleted but the reference to it in the database is still there. When you don't find a page there isn't too much you can do about it (unless you use Google http://www.google.com – it caches all pages it finds).

WHAT SEARCH SITES WON'T FIND

Even the largest of the search sites on the Web index less than 20% of the Web's contents. Here is what is not indexed or searchable through Web search sites:

- PDF (Portable Document Format) and formatted files: References to Adobe Acrobat (.pdf) files or other graphics will be found, but the actual content of these types of documents won't be indexed.
- Content in sites requiring a log in: Web indexing can't get behind a registration screen so, for example, content on *The New York Times* won't be indexed.
- Some content in frames and image maps: Some of the formatting techniques on Web pages will make indexing impossible.
- CGI output: CGI (Common Gateway Interface) is a way Web sites allow people to search the contents of the Web site. A search is entered and the CGI output is the result of the search. These are done on the fly, so they cannot be indexed and found in a Web search.
- Content in databases on the Web site: There might be a wonderful database on a Web site but you won't find what is actually in it through a Web search. Gary Price, of George Washington University, has put together a useful compilation of more than 1000 databases on the Web where you can hunt down some things spiders won't be able to, **Direct Search:** *http://gwis2.circ.gwu.edu/~gprice/direct.htm*
- Intranet pages: Pages that sit behind a "firewall" on a corporate server aren't indexed.
- Sites with robots.txt file to keep files off limits: Web page designers can add a code to certain pages or files they don't want Web search site indexing to pick up.

WEB SEARCH SITES

Now that we've looked at the basics of searching, we need to talk about where to apply these searching skills.

According to one estimate, there are more than 1,500 search services on the World Wide Web, and it seems there is a new one announced every day. If you count the number of sites which compile directories or lists of links to Web sites there would be tens of thousands of Web site finding aids.

Most of these search services are free to the user. They make their money through selling ads or offering additional premium services. Some charge Web sites that want to be listed in their directory or database, and Web site administrators pay because they want people to find their sites.

These tens of thousands of Web site finding aids break down into eight types.

- Human-indexed – omni guides
- Human-indexed – subject specific
- Spider/robot-indexed – omni guides
- Spider/robot-indexed – subject specific
- Non-Web resource search sites
- Meta search-omni and subject specific
- Web rings
- New types of search sites

The lines between these types can be pretty fuzzy. Some robot sites for Web searching also have human-indexed guides (i.e., Go: *http://www.go. com*). Some robot sites will search for Web pages and for other Internet protocol items, like newsgroup messages or ftp files, or search in archives of articles (i.e., Northern Light: *http://www.northernlight.com)*.

You need to understand how the different types of search sites were created, where the database of information about Web pages and sites comes from, the range, and limitations of the different databases.

You also need to understand that it is impossible to understand the ins and outs of all of the major search services. My advice is to think of search services like I think of friends. It is better to know and understand a few really well so you can depend on them than to know many but only superficially.

So, go visit a number from each of the following categories, but select just a few you really want to get to know.

In this chapter we will look at the eight different types of Web search sites and discuss their general characteristics. We will also look at the differences between the sites that fall into that category. I will not try to profile individual sites. There are some great books and Web sites that do that (see bibliography in the margins). I will list 5-10 of the sites that fall into that category so you can make some visits and look them over yourself.

For each of the search site categories we'll look at:

- **What they are and how they are created:** An overview of the process for getting information about Web sites into this kind of service and how the service works.
- **How much of the Web they index and turnaround time:** A very rough idea of the scope of their indexing of the 800 million or so in-

SOURCES

"Choose the best search engine for your information needs":
http://www.nueva.pvt.k12.ca.us/~debbie/library/research/adviceengine.html#broad
 A nice little chart that gives you some tips on where to go if you are trying to do certain kinds of searches.

BOOKS:

How to Search the Web: A Quick-Reference Guide to Finding Things on the World Wide Web, 2nd Edition. by Robert S. Want (Editor). Want Pub., 1999.

Searching Smart on the World Wide Web: Tools and Techniques for Getting Quality Results, by Cheryl Gould. Library Solutions Press, 1998.

The Information Specialist's Guide to Searching & Researching on the Internet and the World Wide Web, by Ernest Ackermann and Karen Hartman. ABF Content, 1999.

Internet Handbook for Writers, Researchers, and Journalists, by Mary McGuire, Linda Stilborne, Melinda McAdams, Laurel Hyatt. Trifolium Books, 1997.

NEWSLETTERS

The AlterNETive Searcher: The Newsletter of Cost-Effective Web Searching
http://www.hermograph.com/as
678-445-4189 $99/yr
 News of less expensive alternatives to higher-priced resources. Monitors periodical archives and Web-based databases, business information sites and scientific databanks to find bargains.

BiblioData's Price Watcher
www.bibliodata.com
781-444-1154 $169/yr ($129 for nonprofits and individuals)
 Tracks current price announcements. Contains price comparisons, low-cost searching tricks and tips for the major online vendors as well as Web sources. Gives tips for negotiating good rates from vendors of information products.

The Cyberskeptics Guide to Internet Research
http://www.bibliodata.com
781-444-1154 $149/yr ($99 for nonprofits and individuals)
 Evaluates important sites and strategies to help you use the Internet as a serious and cost-effective tool for research. Geared toward business research, market research and competitive intelligence.

SOURCES

*Accessibility and distribution of information on the Web, by Steve Lawrence and Lee Giles: *http://wwwmetrics.com*

dexable pages on the Web* and of the frequency of updating the database with new entries or validity checks of entries currently in the database. Most of the figures used in this section of the profiles comes from Search Engine Watch, the most comprehensive guide to the who, what, when, where, whys and hows of search engines: *http://www.searchenginewatch.com* This type of information is the hardest to be exact about because the competitive nature of the search site business makes this strategic information.

- **When to use them:** A note about the usefulness of this particular type of search site for different research needs.
- **What you are searching in the database:** What are the actual contents of the database you are searching on the site, how much and what type of information is there on the entries about Web sites or pages in the database.
- **Strengths:** What is particularly good about this type of search site.
- **Weaknesses:** What to look out for when using this type of search site.
- **Other features commonly offered:** What else you can do on these kinds of sites.
- **Examples of sites:** Names and Web addresses of 5-10 of these types of sites.
- **Exercises:** A few sample questions to try your hand at using these types of sites (refer back to the searching basics chapter for more about specifics of searching).

HUMAN INDEXED – OMNI GUIDES

In the beginning there was Yahoo! Begun in April 1994 by two Stanford electrical engineering students, David Filo and Jerry Yang, as a way to track the interesting Web sites that were starting to be on the World Wide Web. It has grown into the most phenomenal success story on the Web and has spawned hundreds of wanna-bes.

What they are and how they are created

Human-indexed search sites like Yahoo! are subject-organized directories of Web sites. Web sites entered into the directory have been found by the search site creators or have been submitted for indexing and addition to the directory by the submitting site's administrator. When a site has been found or is submitted humans assign hierarchical subject categories to the entry about the site which then becomes part of the search site's database.

I refer to these as "omni guides" because they cover the entire range of subjects represented on the Web. They are trying to index Web pages on aardvarks to Zulus and everything in-between.

How much of the Web they index and turnaround time

Because of the labor-intensity of human indexing, these kinds of sites cover the lowest percentage of indexable Web pages. The largest of these types of services, Yahoo! has only 1 million sites listed.

What is in the database you are searching

You are searching on the subject terms used to describe the page or site, the title and address of the Web site and, sometimes, a brief description of the contents of the site. They do not index every word on the page.

If, for example, you are looking for information on the decadal survey the American Astronomical Society is conducting, a search of "decadal survey" in Yahoo! will not turn up the AAS Web site. The entry for the AAS only says: "The major professional organization in North America for astronomers and other scientists and individuals interested in astronomy" so the search engine can't find anything on "decadal survey" in the database. This gets confusing. If Yahoo! can't find anything in it's database, it automatically searches the Inktomi database which DOES index every word through it's robot and gives you the results of that search – but it's not coming from Yahoo!

In human-indexed sites, you can use search the database or just click through the subject categories from broad terms to narrower and narrower categorizations. This is said to be a site which is "searchable" and "browsable".

Strengths

- The careful categorization puts some organizational structure to the indexing of the Web.
- Some human-indexed search sites are very selective about the sites they put in the index, the sites you are sent to tend to be of higher quality.
- Some have ratings for sites in the index based on different criteria.

Weaknesses

- Very limited coverage of the Web's contents.
- Little information about the sites on which to search, not deeply indexed.
- No focus, trying to cover all topics.
- A Web site can be indexed under multiple subjects, there can be duplication of results.
- Some index sites are starting to charge Web sites for better placement in the index so returns might be based on $, not relevance.

When to use them

When you are just looking for a sampling of good sites on a broad topic. Don't use them if you are looking for very specific terms or people (unless the people are celebrities or well-known).

Other features commonly offered

Many of these sites are becoming "portals" – doorways to all the features and functions of the Web. They will offer e-mail, ads, news, and different subject "channels". Some are affiliated with other search services (i.e., Yahoo! and Inktomi).

Examples of sites

- Britannica: *http://www.britannica.com* From the Encyclopedia Britannica, sites in the index are given from one to five stars based on quality of the information.

"Knowledge is of two kinds; we know a subject ourselves, or we know where we can find information upon it."

Samuel Johnson, 1775

- InfoMine: *http://infomine.ucr.edu/* Aimed at academic research needs.
- Magellan Internet Guide: *http://magellan.excite.com/* The indexed directory affiliated with the Excite robot search site.
- Snap: *http://www.snap.com*
- World Wide Web Virtual Library: *http://www.vlib.org*
- Yahoo!: *http://www.yahoo.com*

Exercises

- Think of a fairly broad topic. Go to three of the human-indexed directory sites listed above and browse through the subject listings for that topic, how do the subject categories used in the various sites differ?
- A Krishna temple is opening in town. Where can you go to find Web sites about Hare Krishna?
- You want information about violence in middle and high schools. Find relevant Web sites in Yahoo by browsing through the subject categories. Then do a search in the search box. How did the results differ?

HUMAN-INDEXED – SUBJECT SPECIFIC

Many Web users have seen value of Yahoo-type directories of Web sites but also realize the impossibility of any site doing justice to all subjects. They are turning to subject-specific human-indexed search sites. The best of these follow Yahoo!'s look and style.

What they are and how they are created

They work just the same as the omni-guides, the difference is they concentrate on a single topic.

How much of the Web do they index and turnaround time

Their coverage of the relevant Web sites for a topic is generally more comprehensive than the omni-guides' coverage. Usually, they are more diligent about keeping the index up to date, so they check the currency of sites more frequently.

What is in the database you are searching

The same sort of information as in the omni-guides. These guides are also usually browsable and searchable.

Strengths

- Focused content, the sub-categories can be more specific and defined.
- Site entries are usually well-annotated so you can select which site to use based on a more thorough description.
- Many of these index sites do careful selection of the contents to put in the index. You're likely to get good quality sites.

Weaknesses

- Some subject-specific guides go for quantity, not quality. Find out their submission policy. Do they put any submitted Web site into their directory or are they selective?

- Some of the guides are somebody's hobby, for a while. The Web site compiler might lose interest, so check for the freshness of the listings. When was new material last entered, when were the current entries checked to see if the links were still valid?

READ MORE:

Great Scouts! Cyberguides to subject searching on the Web, by Nora Paul and Margot Williams. Cyberage Books, 1999.

When to use them

When you are focusing on a particular broad topic and want to find good content sites on that topic.

Other features commonly offered

There are often content areas on these search sites with compilations of documents or background material relevant to the subject (i.e., a legal dictionary and database search of the U.S. Constitution on the FindLaw site.)

Examples of sites:

- FindLaw: *http://www.findlaw.com* Legal information.
- Landings: *http://www.landings.com* Aviation information (find the aviation directory at the bottom of the page).
- Officer.com: *http://www.officer.com/* Police officer links.
- Virtual Religion Index: *http://religion.rutgers.edu/links/vrindex.html* Religion links from Rutgers. Browsable but not searchable.
- Envirolink: *http://www.envirolink.org/* Enviromental resources.
- LatinoWeb: *http://www.latinoweb.com* Latino/Hispanic resources.
- Medical Matrix: *http://www.medmatrix.org* You have to register to use this site which has a well organized collection of medical and health links.

Collections of Subject-Specific Directories

- Argus Clearinghouse: *http://www.clearinghouse.net/* A collection of subject-specific guides submitted to the Clearinghouse evaluated by the Argus team.
- About.com: *http://www.about.com* More than 600 hosted subject guides on thousands of topics.

Exercises

- You are working on a story about hazardous waste transportation issues. Look in Envirolink for resources, then look in one of the omniguides. Which one had more references? Which had more relevant sources? Which was easier to use?
- You have to cover the unveiling of a new memorial to police who have been killed in the line of duty. Where might you find some background information on other police memorials in the U.S.?
- Your city's airport press agents proudly announce the signing on of the 86th airline to bring service to their facility. In the press release it says, "This makes the number of airlines using our airport even larger than London's Heathrow." Are you just going to put that into the news story or are you going to check it out?

ROBOT/SPIDER INDEXED – OMNI GUIDES

What they are and how they are created

Instead of relying on humans to index the Web entries, spider-(also known as robots) indexed search sites rely on software. One of the clearest explanations of how spiders work comes from Danny Sullivan, the master reviewer of search engine technology. This comes from his excellent site Search Engine Watch: *http://www.searchenginewatch.com*

"Search engines have three major elements. First is the spider, also called the crawler. The spider visits a Web page, reads it, and then follows links to other pages within the site. This is what it means when someone refers to a site being 'spidered' or 'crawled.' The spider returns to the site on a regular basis, such as every month or two, to look for changes.

Everything the spider finds goes into the second part of a search engine, the index. The index, sometimes called the catalog, is like a giant book containing a copy of every Web page that the spider finds. If a Web page changes, then this book is updated new information.

Sometimes it can take a while for new pages or changes that the spider finds to be added to the index. Thus, a Web page may have been "spidered" but not yet "indexed." Until it is indexed – added to the index – it is not available to those searching with the search engine.

Search engine software is the third part of a search engine. This is the program that sifts through the millions of pages recorded in the index to find matches to a search and rank them in order of what it believes is most relevant." (*Copyright 1999 internet.com LLC. All Rights Reserved. Used with Permission.*)

How much of the Web do they index and turnaround time

The performance of spider indexing has deteriorated as the Web has grown. In a 1998 article in *Science,* "Searching the World Wide Web" (April, 1998), Steve Lawrence and Lee Giles estimated 320 million indexable pages on the Web and that the most comprehensive search engine covered about 46% of the pages. A new study by Lawrence and Giles (*http://www.metrics.com*) estimates 800 million pages with the best search site covering only 16%.

How often the spider is sent out to capture information to add to the index varies from one search site to another. It can be as often as every few weeks or as infrequently as several months or more.

What is in the database you are searching

The spider captures every page and the indexing software indexes every word on the page (except for so-called stop words, common words like "the", "and", "a". Different search engines have different sets of stop words.). The Web address, Web page title, and "meta-tags" are also indexed. (Meta-tags are words added to the coding of a site that provides keywords and descriptions of the site that can be read by the indexing software but which aren't seen on the Web page itself. This is why you sometimes get sites, usually porno sites, that don't match what you are searching. The Web page creator throws all kinds of words into the meta-tags hoping people searching on one of the words will get their Web site in the results.)

Some of the search engines don't actually index every word on the page, they may just do the first dozen or so lines. It is important to read the documentation.

Strengths

- The thoroughness of the indexing: much of the page is indexed instead of just a description.
- The coverage of the Web: a larger slice of the Web's contents are indexed.
- The ability to find specific words and names located deep within a Web page.
- The relevancy ranking feature of most of the search engines brings the best of the results to the top.
- Some of the search sites tie in the items in their subject directory to the general spider search results. In Go, for example, a search of "jungle" got 563,483 results, but at the top of the page was "Matching Topics" (from their subject directory): it had links to such items as Jungle Music, Upton Sinclair, Brendan Fraser, Wildcats, Cannibalism. Each of these items had links to 4-5 Web sites.

Weaknesses

- The good, bad and the ugly of the Web are all mixed together in the database, there is no quality control.
- The results list is sometimes overwhelming, there are so many hits.
- The indexing can be out of date, items you click to from the results list may no longer be on the Web.
- Going from one spider search site to another can be confusing, they use different commands and have different features.
- Search flexibility is not as great as with commercial services. Few of the search sites have, for example, the ability to build on a previous search called "nesting the search." (Nesting the search allows one to do a search and then modify it to add another term or to search within the results of the previous search you did. Go is one of the few which do offer that function.)
- Many of them offer so many other features, it is hard to find the basic search functions within the search site's page.

When to use them

- If you are going for a specific, rather than a broad topic. For broad topics, finding sites under subject categories in a human-indexed directory might be better.
- If a search in a human-indexed directory did not find anything.
- If you are going for a more comprehensive search and want to find a lot of the available resources about that topic.

Other features commonly offered

Many spider search sites are also offering Yahoo-like directories of Web sites with much more selective lists of Web sites on a topic. Many will have searches of other Internet functions available in addition to the Web page search, they will have newsgroup message searches or ftp searches, for example. Most have shopping "channels" and other transaction features.

Examples of sites

- AltaVista: *http://www.altavista.com* Considered to be the largest spider site.
- Excite: *http://www.excite.com*

- HotBot: *http://www.hotbot.com* Searches for types of files (photo, audio, etc.)
- Go: *http://www.go.com* Formerly known as Infoseek (name changed in May 1999). One of the best features is you can build on a search. Search a topic and then search for another word within the results from the previous search.
- Lycos: *http://www.lycos.com*
- Northern Light: *http://www.northernlight.com* Web search and search archive of magazine and news stories.

Exercises

- You are going to be interviewing a world-renowned cytologist. You must have missed class the day they talked about that in school and aren't really sure what a cytologist does. Where can you find some information about cytology and come up with some good questions to ask her?
- You are looking for the text of the Universal Human Rights bill, or something like that. You aren't sure of the exact name of it. Can you find it? It's pretty old, from the '40s or '50s and it was some kind of United Nations thing.
- Do a search on your state. You get so many hits, you want to narrow it down. Find Web pages that mention your state and crime.
- You sometimes get these strange messages when you click to a site on a set of results, stuff like 404 Not Found, or Connection Refused by Host. Find a listing and explanation of Internet error messages.
- Does anyone sell manure on the Web? (No, real manure, from farm animals.)

ROBOT/SPIDER-INDEXED – SUBJECT SPECIFIC

What they are and how they are created

They work just the same as the general spider search sites, the difference is they concentrate on a single topic. Instead of sending their spider out to roam the entire Web, they select specific Web sites or domains they send the spider out to. Most countries now have a spider search site which only looks at and indexes Web sites in that country.

How much of the Web do they index and turnaround time

Their coverage of the Web sites they selected for indexing for a topic is much more comprehensive. They usually index deeper into the selected sites and they send the spider out more frequently so the index is usually much more up to date. Some, like the news site spiders, index Web site contents several times a day.

What is in the database you are searching

Same as with the spider sites that range the Web, the database indexes all the words on the Web pages the spider has crawled.

Strengths

- Subject focus makes the hits much more relevant; you know they are coming from a site that has been pre-selected.

- The currency of the database is usually better, fewer dead links to pages that are no longer there.
- If you are looking for information from a specific country, finding one of the country specific search engines really narrows down the results.

Weaknesses

- Might be too narrow, might miss sites with sections that would be relevant to the subject but aren't totally about the subject.

When to use them

When you are interested in a particular subject or type of material and only want to get information from sites that focus on that. When you want to make sure you will be getting relevant information, filtered by the spider's destination list.

Examples of sites

- LawCrawler: *http://lawcrawler.findlaw.com* Specific spiders sent out to international sites, USA, and specific state law and government sites. Uses AltaVista search engine.
- Medical World Search: *http://www.enigma.co.nz/mws/index.html* "100,000 Web pages from thousands of selected medical sites."
- GovBot: *http://ciir2.cs.umass.edu/Govbot/* Use the form to search in 1 million plus Web pages from U.S. Government and Military sites around the country.
- Pinstripe: *http://pinstripe.opentext.com/* Business information.
- TotalNews: *http://www.totalnews.com* Ranges through news Web sites and brings you current news which hits the subject you search.
- Regional spider search sites from Search Engine Watch: *http://www.searchenginewatch.com/facts/regional/index.html* Not only is this a great listing, there is also a great explanation of how regional spiders work.

Exercises

- You get a tip that a legislator in your state who had been arrested and convicted a few years back had his record expunged. Where can you find information about what expunging a record means?
- You're doing a series on gun control and you want to keep up with what kinds of stories other news organizations have been doing on it. Where could you go to find some recent stories on gun control?
- There's a new release about radon levels in the air and water in your region. You've got the environmental information, but you need to know more about the health effects. Find some medical sites with information about radon.

NON-WEB RESOURCE SEARCH SITES

What they are and how they are created

These are Web sites for finding resources other than Web pages. These are the kinds of finding aids described in the sections about newsgroups, discussion lists, ftp, telnet, and gopher.

What is in the database you are searching

It depends on the kind of protocol they are helping you locate. News-group message locators will index the text of the message. Discussion list finders will just have brief descriptions of the discussion lists.

Strengths

The focus on specific types of Internet resources can help when you are looking for a certain non-Web resource. These may be the only way to efficiently find these kinds of resources.

Weaknesses

Some of the less used protocols on the Internet (telnet or ftp, for example) might not have protocol finding aids that are up-to-date or comprehensive.

When to use them

When you are looking for something other than a Web page or Web site.

Examples of sites

- Deja: *http://www.deja.com* Find newsgroups and newsgroup messages.
- Topica: *http://www.topica.com* Find e-mail discussion lists.
- Filez: *http://www.filez.com* Find ftp-able files.

Exercises

Look in the chapters on newsgroups, discussion lists, ftp and telnet to find some exercises.

META-SEARCH SITES

What they are and how they are created

Think of meta-search sites as one-stop search sites. They don't create their own indexes of information about Web pages. They send out the search you put into the meta-search site and submit it to all the other search sites which then search their own indexes and send back the results. You'll get a compilation of the results coming from the different search sites.

How much of the Web do they index and turnaround time

Because they combine the results from a number of different spider and human-indexed directories, doing a meta-search is probably one of the most comprehensive searches. Still not the whole Web, but it may snag things collectively that you wouldn't have gotten individually.

What is in the database you are searching

The database contents will be the same as for the spider search.

Strengths

- Enter one search, get results back from multiple search sites' indexes.
- Gets the best results from the different indexes quickly and easily.

Weaknesses

- Some major search sites aren't available on meta-search pages (i.e., HotBot).
- Searches can time out if the search site the search is sent to doesn't respond quickly. It will come back saying there were no results, but that doesn't mean there is nothing on that topic at the site.
- The search refinement features (like phrase searching or boolean connectors) are often stripped in the translation to different search sites. Searching is less precise than going to the individual sites and searching.
- Most meta-search sites don't filter the results to remove duplicates. You'll get multiple hits of the same sites.

When to use them

When you've got a specific, obscure topic and want to fling the net out widely. Also useful for doing a broad search and scanning the top results from a variety of search sites.

Other features commonly offered

They often will search other databases than just Web pages (newsgroup messages, ftp files, newswires…)

Examples of sites

- Dogpile: *http://www.dogpile.com* Searches 26 search sites, three at a time.
- Inference Find: *http://www.infind.com* Searches the 6 major sites and retrieves all the results from each.
- Debriefing: *http://www.debriefing.com* Removes duplicates from search results.
- MetaCrawler: *http://www.go2net.com/search.html/*
- Savvy Search: *http://www.savvysearch.com* Select a category to search and the search will go out to a number of related sites.
- ProSeek: *http://www.proseek.net* You can select the region of the world you want to search.
- Web Taxi: *http://www.webtaxi.com* Overcomes the problem of stripping the search strategy (like " " or + signs) by giving options for different search sites they go to.
- MESA: *http://mesa.rrzn.uni-hannover.edu* A specialty search engine which takes a name and searches it in a number of the email-finder services.

Exercise

Try some of the searches you did in other exercises in the meta-search engines. What did you find that you didn't get before?

WEB RINGS

What they are and how they are created

Web rings are an affiliation of related types of Web sites. They are, in some ways, like a consortium of Web sites on related topics. They support each other by providing links from one site to the next in the Web ring.

How much of the Web do they index and turnaround time

They don't index Web sites, they link Web sites.

What is in the database you are searching

The main Web ring search site (*http://www.webring.org*) has descriptions of the Web rings.

Strengths

- You'll often find the more esoteric and fringe types of sites affiliated here, the ones that might not get noticed by the big search site indexes.
- It's easy to hop around from one site to the next to get a sense of the information they have.
- Many support group and personal page sites link together in Web rings. These can be a good way to find personal story pages, people with experience (but not necessarily expertise).

Weaknesses

- You can't search the contents of the pages on the Web rings, just the descriptions of the ring.
- You can't really tell what site will be next in the chain when you click on the Web ring label.
- Most of the sites on Web rings are personal pages, coming from individuals who can, and do, say anything. Use content from these sites with caution, and follow-up by traditional reporting techniques (i.e., call them and interview them and then check out what they say).

When to use them

When you are wandering and want to find a number of similar sites easily. These rings make it easy to travel from one to the next.

The site for finding Web rings

- WebRing: *http://www.webring.org* There is a subject categorized index and a searchable database of Web ring descriptions. Search a topic, and click on one of the Web ring names and get a list of all the Web sites on the ring.

Examples of Web rings

(these are the home sites, the starting points of the ring)

- Native American Ring: *http://www.geocities.com/RainForest/Vines/2063/nativesring.html* More than 665 sites on this ring
- Anorexia and Bulimia Ring: *http://www.geocities.com/HotSprings/2994/*
- Adoption Activism Web Ring: *http://www.geocities.com/Heartland/Plains/5012/adopact.html*
- Channel Zero, the Underground Newspaper Ring: *http://www.oblivion.net/~ugpapers/*

Exercises

- You are doing a story about a child with neurofibromatosis. You want to see if others have been through similar situations that this family has been through. Find some personal pages of neurofibromatosis sufferers.

- There is going to be a James Dean film festival next weekend. You want to interview some fans of the long-dead movie star. Can you find any Dean fanatics?

SOURCES

ARTICLE:

"Search, and Now you Find the Right Stuff," by Margot Williams. *Washington Post,* Feb. 22, 1999. *http://directhit.com/press/articles/ Wash_Post2.html*

NEW TYPES OF SEARCH SITES

Every week, it seems, there is a new search site available on the Web. But most are just another human-indexed directory or another spider search. Some search software is trying to break out from the "spider and index" or the "submit and categorize" approach to searching. Here are some new approaches to finding and pointing you to the Web content that you are looking for.

- **Links spider:** Google: *http://www.google.com* Google's spider doesn't go out and index the contents of Web pages, it indexes where Web pages link to. Huhn? Google figures the best pages on a topic are probably the ones that most people link to from their own Web pages. So, when you do a search on Google, the results are ranked by the pages or sites that other Web sites link to the most.

  Another great feature of Google is that they have "cached" pages they have indexed so even if you find a page in the results which, when you click to it, says the file is not found (it has been removed from the original Web site), just click on the "cached" link under the entry and get a copy of the page as indexed by Google. This is an amazing service.

  This really is a clever approach and is successful in it's mission of giving you the most highly recommended sites. Give it a try.

- **Recommendation engine:** Alexa: *http://www.alexa.com* Alexa is a program you download and add to your browser. When it is running, it automatically links you to the Internic registration information (the registry of who has been issued the Web site address you are looking at, more about that in the credibility checking section). It also has a recommendation database. It keeps track of where Alexa users went to after they had been at the site you linked to and gives you those links. If you liked this site, Alexa figures, you'll like these other sites, too.

- **User popularity tracker**: Direct Hit: *http://www.directhit.com* Let's let them explain what Direct Hit search technology does: "Our Popularity Engine™ tracks the amount of time spent at sites that people actually select from the search results list. By analyzing the activity of millions of previous Internet searchers, Direct Hit determines the most popular and relevant sites for your search request." Direct Hit is the default search engine used on the HotBot search site. Several other search sites are using this technology, too.

  These, and other new approaches to indexing the contents of the Web, are worth keeping an eye on.

Tips:

- On some search services, when you click on one of retrieved items, the results are brought into a "frame" within the search service page. They do this to keep searchers within their service, not send them out to another site. The trouble with this is you can't tell the Web address of the site you've been linked to and you can't bookmark the site, you are just bookmarking the search service's address. To overcome this, if you are using Navigator, have your cursor in the frame with the page you want and click on the right mouse button. Select "Open frame in a new window." It will spawn a new browser and take you to the site which you can then navigate through and bookmark.

- There are thousands of helpful pages about search sites and search engine features. If you only have time for one, and you really want to understand how these types of sites work, go to Search Engine Watch: *http://www.searchenginewatch.com* You'll need nothing else.

SAVING AND REUSING INFORMATION FROM WEB PAGES

The different elements on a Web page come in a variety of formats. There will be photos, audio files, documents, and text. You will sometimes want to take information found on a Web page and use it in a different way. This can include wanting to put the text in an Adobe Acrobat document (files with a .pdf at the end) into a word processor or a table of numbers into a spreadsheet program. You may just want to copy some of the text on a Web page and move it into a word processor.

Here are some of the types of information and files found on Web pages and the techniques you'd use to save them and reuse them. This section will, by no means, provide all the steps and details, but I will give you some resources that you can go to for more help.

One of the first ones that will be helpful is this, on file format. It is no longer updated, but it gives the basic file types and useful information on how to read them. Common Internet File Formats: *http://www.matisse.net/ files/formats.html*

Here are a few of the basic saving and reusing tasks you might find yourself doing on the Web.

Saving a portion of text on a Web page

You locate a speech given by someone you are covering and want to put a portion of the speech text into your story. Don't re-type, just copy and paste.

- Put the cursor at the start of the text you want to copy.
- Click the right mouse button and drag the cursor across the lines you want to copy. They will be highlighted.
- Click the "Edit" on the browser menu bar, select "copy".
- Go to your word processor, put the cursor where you want the text to appear.
- Click the "Edit" on the menu bar, select "paste" and your selected text will be on the page.

Saving a Web page (.htm or .html)

If you find a Web page with great information (and it might not remain on that site forever) you might want to save it so you can reload it later.

- Click on "File" on the browser menu bar
- Go down to "Save as" in the pull-down box
- You'll get a box asking where to save it (on a disk in the A: drive, to your hard drive C:) and what you want to call it.
- Click the "Save" button.

Reusing a saved page in the browser software

- Click on "File"
- Go down to "Open Page" in the pull-down box
- Put in the location of the file that you saved
- Click on "Open" and the page will appear on the browser.

Reusing a saved page in word processing

- You can open a .htm document in your word processing software by opening it up like you would any word document. Then you can copy and paste sections of the page onto another page.

Saving and reusing an Adobe Acrobat document

Many government and commercial sites use .PDF (portable document format) files to provide copies of documents. .PDF files maintain the original formatting of the document and will display charts, signatures and other information from the original document. .PDF files require Adobe Acrobat software, a free reader program, to display the files. Once you download the reader (*http://www.adobe.com/prodindex/acrobat/readstep.html*) into your browser, you will be able to open up any .PDF file.

You might want to copy some of the text or numbers found on a .PDF file into a word processor or spreadsheet. This can be tricky but here are some of the techniques you can try. Debbie Wolfe, newsroom technology training editor at the *St. Petersburg Times*, has put together a tip sheet on saving and moving information from Adobe Acrobat documents:

Debbie Wolfe's Adobe Tip Sheet

When you find a **".pdf"** file at a Web site, download it to your hard drive (see the how-to steps below) and then open the document in the Acrobat Reader software – INDEPENDENT OF *ANY* WEB BROWSER WINDOW! (To practice, check out regional AIDS data at the Statistical Rolodex site: **http://www.cdc.gov/nchswww/fastats/fastats.htm**)

Within Acrobat Reader you will have choices. You can print the document in whole or in part. You can copy the document in whole or in part and paste it into a word processing screen, like Word97, so the data can be saved as a text file. Numerical data in Acrobat Reader must be saved first as a text file before importing it into Excel97 for data analysis. ***Text can be copied from Acrobat Reader and pasted directly into Excel97.***

1. RIGHT-mouse click on the Web link that leads to the Acrobat Reader file – a pop-up menu will appear; LEFT-mouse click on "Save Target As…"
2. In the "Save As" window use the down-arrow in the "Save in:" box to select the folder where you wish to save the file (Extra tip: Change the drive letter from "C" to "A" to save to your floppy disk…instead of the hard drive.)
3. In the "File name:" box, give the file a name that reflects the contents (do not type a period and three-character extension – let the software assign this part of the file name)
4. In the "Save as type:" box make sure it says: Adobe Acrobat Document
5. Click on the "Save" button; the file will be saved to your hard drive with a ".pdf" extension (Earlier versions of Excel work similarly.)

To copy an *entire page* in Acrobat Reader to a word processing window

(Word, WordPad, etc.) so you can save the page as a Word ".doc" or text ".txt" file:

1. Display the page you want to copy then click "Edit" on the menu bar; click on "Select all" from the drop-down menu.

2. Switch to a Windows word processing program, like Microsoft Word, where you can then paste the data into a new or existing document (click on "Edit"; click on "Paste"). Save it as a ".doc" file if you plan to use the data as a word processing file. For use in Excel, you **must** save the word processing file (click on "File"; click on "Save as") as a text file (**numbers.txt** as opposed to **numbers.doc**) by selecting the "text" option in the "Save as type:" window. In the "Look in:" box, click the down-arrow to choose a folder or use the nearby icon to create a new folder. Save the file and **CLOSE IT** before trying to open the text file in Excel.

To copy a _portion of a page_ in Acrobat Reader to a word processing window (WordPad, Word, etc.) so you can save the data as a Word ".doc" or text ".txt" file:

1. Display the page that contains the data (a column of numbers, a table of numbers, a footnote, a column of labels) you want to copy. Click on "Tools" on the menu bar; click on "Select Text" from the drop-down menu.
2. _Hold down_ the "Ctrl" key on the keyboard and drag your mouse around the data area you wish to copy; release the mouse button and the "Ctrl" key (notice the data is now highlighted); click on "Edit"; click on "Copy."
3. Switch to a Windows word processing program, like Microsoft Word, where you can then paste the data into a new or existing document (click on "Edit;" click on "Paste"). Save it as a ".doc" file if you plan to use the data as a word processing file. For use in Excel, you **must** save the word processing file (click on "File"; click on "Save as") as a text file (**numbers.txt** as opposed to **numbers.doc**) by selecting the "text" option in the "Save as type:" window. In the "Look in:" box, click the down-arrow to choose a folder or use the nearby icon to create a new folder. Save the file and **CLOSE IT** before trying to open the text file in Excel.

To open a text (numbers.txt) file in Excel:

1. Open Excel. Within Excel, click on "File" on the menu bar; click on "Open" and select the file you just saved in the "text" format. You will probably need to tell Excel what folder to "Look in" and you will need to tell it to either display "Text" or "All Files (*.*)" in the "Files of type:" box. Once you locate the file, open it.
2. When Excel opens a ".txt" file it will present you with the "Text Import Wizard – Step 1 of 3" window. In the area labeled "Original data type" make sure the black dot is in the circle next to the "Delimited" option – click in a circle to move the black dot from one location to another; click on the "Next" button. (A delimiter is a character that separates the parts of your data. For instance, a space is the delimiter between the words and punctuation that comprise this handout.)
3. In the "Text Import Wizard – Step 2 of 3" window, look in the "Delimiters" area and click in the box next to the delimiter that best fits your data. HINT: The words in a text file are generally separated with _spaces_ as opposed to _commas_ or _tabs_ or _semi-colons_). Watch the preview screen in the wizard as you place check marks next to the various delimiter choices. You can select more than one delimiter but generally you will either need to click next to "Space" or "Comma." Click on the "Finish" button.

4. When you save the Excel file for the first time after using the Import Wizard, click on "File"; click on "Save As." In the "Save as type:" box, click on "Microsoft Excel Workbook (*.xls)" – it's the top option. Now your file name will look like: numbers.xls and the last thing you need to do is click the "Save" button.

Saving and reusing a graphic (picture of a spreadsheet table or chart)

If you find a photo or graphic you'd like to save, click on the right mouse button, move down to "Save image as", clicking on this will pull up the box to indicate where to save it and what name to save it as. Then you can open it up later by inserting it into a word processing document.

Saving and reusing a database from a Web site

Most statistical files found on Web sites are .xls files – Excel spreadsheet format. When you find these, you can download them into your Excel spreadsheet by saving the file and then opening it as you would any workbook in the Excel software. There are excellent books about using Excel which will cover these functions.

More information about file types and importing Web information:

- *Computer Assisted Reporting: A practical guide,* 2nd ed. By Brant Houston. Bedford/St. Martin's, 1999. This has an excellent section on importing data into spreadsheets.
- Multimedia File Formats on the Internet: *http://www.lib.rochester. edu/multimed/contents.htm*

   "This is a beginner's guide to file formats on the Internet. It is intended to cover the most basic concepts of various file formats available on the Internet, and the ways to identify and to use the files. It was planned to function as an "one stop shopping" guide for IBM PC compatible users who have some knowledge of DOS and Windows." This is a little dated, but provides an excellent overview and tips for how to recognize and download Internet files.

Types of Material Online: Comparisons of Commercial Services and Web Sites

So far, most of this guide has been talking about the Internet and, more specifically, the World Wide Web. This is appropriate since the Web has become the information utility most available to and used by journalists and researchers.

But we need to talk about commercial services, too. Text archives and public records databases for which you need a subscription are bread-and-butter resources for information professionals and news researchers. Although many of them have migrated to Web-based interfaces (you don't need to dial out to their computer, you can go through the Internet), they are a somewhat different breed than the Web sites we've been talking about.

The first shots of the information revolution came from commercial database services. Defined as "a collection of data or body of information that is organized for rapid retrieval via a computer," databases have been the foundation of computer-assisted research since the late 1970s.

Commercial database services act as agents for the individual databases developed by database producers (such as government agencies, newspapers, magazines, and associations). They are the vendors of the data to the public, offering computer space, search software, marketing and access in exchange for part of the revenue generated by people using the database.

In the age of the Web, many of these database producers have started to cut out the commercial vendor "middleman". They are selling access to their archives and databases directly to the information consumer on their Web site.

This is good news in that the cost of database searching is usually considerably cheaper through the producer's Web site than through a commercial "re-seller". The bad news, though, is the loss of the convenience of one-stop searching. On commercial services one search hits lots of files. There are some Web search sites which are trying to provide that sort of service, but with limited success.

In this section we will discuss the different types of material that can be found in commercial databases and compare these services to Web resources that retrieve the same types of materials. For the most part, the commercial services we will discuss are the "Big Three" text archives (Dialog, Nexis/Lexis, Dow Jones News Retrieval) and public records databases.

Many university and public libraries are making access to the commercial databases they subscribe to available through their Web sites. Usually, however, this service is only available to registered users (students, faculty, or library card holders).

Here are the types of information available on commercial database services, how they compare with Web-based access to these materials, and how they can be used in newsroom research and reporting. Individual databases consist of one or more of the following types of information:

SOURCES

GALE DIRECTORY OF DATABASES – 99th *edition.* Gale Group, 1998. In book or CD-Rom. Profiles more than 13,000 databases from around the world. Find information at The Gale Group: *http://www.gale.com*

Information Today
Searcher
  Find information about these two magazines and selected articles from past issues at
http://www.infotoday.com

EContent Database Online
Online
  Find information about these two magazines at
http://www.onlineinc.com

- Bibliographic citations and abstracts
- Articles and transcripts
- Books and directories
- Government documents
- Public records and consumer records
- Photos and graphics

First, a word about the cost of commercial databases

Commercial database vendors on and off the Web have been scrambling to figure out ways to keep their services competitive. Many services which were transactional cost based (you paid for the amount of time you were online) are going to a flat-rate subscription. Some let you search for free but you pay per article you want to read. Others charge a different fee for the retrieval of different kinds of documents (particularly true with public records). These payment options, and the variety of sources available for finding the same kind of information, make careful shopping for information even more important.

BIBLIOGRAPHIC CITATIONS AND ABSTRACTS

The first databases available commercially were bibliographic or abstract based. These databases provide references to articles available in thousands of publications. Bibliographic citations give only author, title, and publication information, while abstract citations also give a synopsis of the contents of the article. Most of these databases use a set of keywords or controlled vocabulary terms to aid in searching. Most producers of bibliographic or abstract databases focus on a particular subject area.

Examples of bibliographic and abstract databases

- **Cancerlit:** Over 1 million citations to cancer studies, articles and treatment reports dating back to 1963.

- **Dissertation Abstracts:** More than 1.1 million citations to doctoral dissertations from accredited educational institutions. Great for finding experts on esoteric topics.

- **Religion Index:** From the American Theological Library Association, provides citations to articles dating back to 1949 in more than 500 international religion studies journals.

- **Social Scisearch:** The Institute for Scientific Information has pulled together these cites from 1,500 social science journals since 1972.

Uses in news research

- **Oldest material:** Bibliographic and citation databases have references to material dating back the furthest. If you want to find a magazine article from the 1960s, you will most likely find a reference to it in a bibliographic database.

- **Esoteric material:** Articles in obscure and special interest magazines are often indexed.

- **Background information:** The abstracts often give you basic information about the topic and lead you to alternative terms to search by.

- **Locate experts:** Writers of articles on specific topics can be great sources. Usually the magazine they wrote for can help you locate the writer.

- **Story ideas:** Just reading through a list of article titles can give you ideas and angles to the topic you may not have thought to pursue.

- **Facts, statistics:** Abstracts from some databases pull the most relevant facts and figures from the article, obviating the need to go to the source article.

Advantages of Bibliographic and Abstract Databases

- One-search access to information on millions of articles in thousands of journals.

- Location of subject specialists by finding authors of articles on specific topics.

- International coverage of topics of the most arcane and specific nature.

- Generally well indexed. Use of subject headings make searching easier.

- Widest range of dates. Usually indexes material dating further back than full-text databases or material on the Web.

- Data is compiled by associations, institutes and organizations which can be contacted for specific help in locating material.

Disadvantages and cautions

- Can be frustrating to find the perfect article, but not be able to get the full-text easily.

- There are so many documents, it is easy to be overwhelmed with your search results unless you clearly target your search request.

- These are labor intensive databases; writing abstracts takes time; there is often a considerable time lag in the posting of information. This will not have quick access to the most current articles.

- Be sure to check whether the database is still active. Some databases are not being added to, but they continue to be searchable.

Where to find Bibliographic and Abstract Databases

Commercial Services
- **Dialog:** *http://www.dialog.com*

On the Web
- **UnCover:** *http://uncweb.carl.org* UnCover is a database of current article information taken from well over 18,000 multidisciplinary journals. UnCover contains brief descriptive information for over 8,800,000 articles which have appeared since Fall 1988. Search for free, articles can be faxed to you.

- **National Agricultural Library** (U.S. Dept. of Agriculture): *http://www.nalusda.gov/isis/* Information about how to telnet to the Journal Article Citation Database, citations to articles back to 1984.

- **GEAC**, a major supplier of library resources, offers a free monthly trial of a featured database. Check out which one is free to try out this month. (It was the Food Science and Technology database in May 1999 – a nice bibliographic database.) *http://webspirs.geac.com.au/fido/*

Search Example and Exercise

- After a TV movie about the transporting of nuclear waste, you decide to do a story and you want some background.

Searching in UnCover, *transporting nuclear waste,* you get this citation:

> Title: For A Few Dollars More: Public Trust and the Case for Transporting Nuclear Waste in Dedicated Trains.
> Author(s): Glickman, Theodore S.
>
> Golding, Dominic
> Journal Info: Policy studies review.: Wint 1991 v 10 n 4 127
>
> (It will cost $20.00 to have it faxed or desktop delivered)

This is probably a good article, but it costs a bit. What other strategy might you use to get some background on this issue?

■ Go to the GEAC site and try out their free database of the month. The search template is interesting and it will help you practice different kinds of search strategies: *http://webspirs.geac.com.au/fido/*

ARTICLES AND TRANSCRIPTS

Also referred to as "full-text" databases, these take you a step further than the bibliographic database by providing you with the complete text of articles, programs, speeches, and press releases. Most databases created since the mid-1980s provide full-text retrieval of material. Some full-text databases contain the text from just one publication, others are compilations of articles from a variety of source publications. Most commercial database services allow you to search for articles across a number of databases with one search, essentially making one huge compilation database from a number of separate databases.

Newspaper archives, which had been available exclusively through commercial database services, are now selling their archives on the Web. Some newspapers, not considered big enough fish to be on the big commercial services, are providing online access to their archives for the first time through their Web site.

There are a couple of services that try to facilitate cross-archive searching on the Web (see below).

Examples of article and transcript databases

■ **AP, TASS, Reuter, Xinhua, States News Services** and other wire services.

■ **Magazine ASAP:** More than 380,000 articles from 100 general interest periodicals, with 3,400 additional records uploaded weekly.

■ **Washington Post, Jerusalem Post, Jakarta Post, Palm Beach Post,** and more than 500 other daily newspapers around the world.

■ **Screen Digest, Insider Trading Monitor, Food Chemical News, Infectious Disease Weekly** and over 4,000 other newsletters and journals.

■ **20/20, 48 Hours, 60 Minutes** and over 120 other news programs from ABC, CBC, CBS, CNN, FNN, NBC, NPR and PBS.

SOURCES

BOOKS

Fulltext Sources Online: for periodicals, newspapers, newsletters, newswires and tv/radio transcripts. Information Today: *http://www. infotoday.com*
Editor: Ruth M. Orenstein
$118.00/yr.
  The best source for seeing clearly the options for accessing over 4,000 periodical titles. Gives the services the database is available on, the file name and the range of dates covered. Geographic and subject indexes add to the usability of this reference.

Net.Journal Directory: The Catalog of Full Text Periodicals Archived on the World Wide Web – Lawrence Krumenaker, Hermograph Press: *http://www.hermograph.com*
$125, annual subscriptions (2 editions) $220, current issue plus 1-year subscription $299
678-445-4189
  Prices, dates of coverage and article formats for over 10,000 full-text publications on over 700 Websites and 28 fee-based Web services. Features sites for newspapers – U.S. and international – and current-issue-only and limited-time archive sites. Includes a guide to the various syntaxes and commands for searching.

Uses in news research

- **Background:** Full text databases of news stories can help track down previous incidents, find background on the people involved in an incident and otherwise put a news story into context. The broad range of publications, and their particular focus, offers articles representing a variety of viewpoints.

- **Scope and range:** The range of sources available in full-text databases makes it possible to put a broader perspective on a local story, or to make an international story relevant to your community.

- **Facts, statistics:** Full text articles from subject-specialty magazines and newsletters can reveal information from reports and studies that may not have gotten into mainstream publications.

- **Story ideas:** As with abstract databases, the articles retrieved can give you ideas about angles to follow in covering your story.

Advantages of Full Text Databases

- **Instant gratification:** You get the whole article immediately.

- **Online library:** You have the text of thousands of magazines, publications, speeches and news programs instantly available.

- **Cost effective:** If you add up what paper subscriptions to these publications would cost, it may be cheaper to just access when you need them. Now with full text archives on the Web, the cost has gotten even lower.

- **International scope:** European, Asian, Australian and Latin American wire services and newspapers are available.

- **Regional information:** Access to a wide range of local newspapers and weekly magazines gives you a regional perspective on people and events.

Disadvantages and cautions

- **Difficult to search:** There is so much material, it is easy to retrieve too many articles.

- **Difficult to search – part 2:** There are so many full-text databases scattered around the Web, it can be frustrating to cover all the bases.

- **Searches what you type, not what you mean:** Full text is searched with the characters in your search statement, not by the meaning of the words you type. In full text, it is easy to have a search for the planet Mercury to retrieve "as the mercury soared to 102 degrees", or "the Mercury Cougar careened into the embankment", or "Mercury Morris will always be remembered", or "the mercury gray siding". Balancing specificity without too tightly narrowing your search is a skill developed over time. Ask your researcher for search strategy help.

- **Duplication of material:** Searching in newspaper files, for example, can retrieve multiple copies of the same article from different newspapers. Some newspapers even put in different editions' versions of the same story, often with little or very subtle changes.

- **Not comprehensive:** Do not assume that if something or someone is not retrieved in a search that there has been nothing written about them. This is a tool of inclusion (if you find it, you can assume it is there), not a tool of exclusion (if you don't find it, you can't assume it doesn't exist).

"It is a very sad thing that nowadays there is so little useless information."

Oscar Wilde

- **Consider the source:** Errors in articles are not always caught. If a piece of information is important to the story you are writing, verify it with another source. You must understand how the articles and the publications are written and how the database is compiled to get the fullest sense of what your search has and has not revealed.

Where to find full text Article and Transcript databases

Commercial Services (all require a subscription – most are now searchable on the Web)

- **Burrelle's Information Services:** *http://www.burrelles.com* Broadcast transcripts from over 160 network and cable stations dating back to 1989. Not searchable on the Web.

- **Datastar:** *http://phoenix.dialog.com/products/datastar/* European business databases, searchable on the Dialog Web site: *http://www.datastarweb.com/*

- **Dialog:** *http://www.dialog.com/* Over 90 U.S. newspapers and 40 non-U.S. papers. Full text to hundreds of specialty magazines. Searchable on the Web.

- **Dow Jones** (Wall St. Journal): *http://www.djnr.com* Access to *The Wall Street Journal* and news wires, business magazines and major newspapers around the world. Searchable on the Web.

- **Lexis/Nexis:** *http://www.lexis-nexis.com/* Over 100 newspapers full text and hundreds of magazine and transcript archives. Massive legal resource databases. Searchable on the Web.

- **NewsBank:** *http://www.newsbank.com/* They've gone from a microfiche-based clipping service to a full fledged database vendor on the Web in the past 25 years. Although the market has traditionally been for schools and public libraries, their Web product is good for companies, too.

- **Congressional Quarterly databases:** *http://www.cq.com* Legislative tracking and news service. Check out the free databases they have available, too.

- **Westlaw:** *http://www.westlaw.com* Legal resources databases.

On the Web

- **Northern Light – Special Collections:** *http://www.northern-light.com* This spider search site also has an archive of articles from 5,000 journals, books, magazines, newspapers, and wires, many of which can't be found anywhere else on the Web. Searching is free, articles you want to read cost from $1 to $4 each.

- **Electric Library:** *http://www.elibrary.com* Select magazines, maps, books & reports, newspapers & news wires, transcripts, or pictures and then select a special subject area. Give the free trial a try. Flat rate subscription for unlimited searching makes this one of the best data deals on the Web.

- **NewsLibrary:** *http://www.newslibrary.com* 65 U.S. newspapers (most Knight-Ridder papers) are searchable for free, read the whole story for $1.00 – $2.95.

- **Internet Prospector: News Online:** *http://w3.uwyo.edu/~prospect/news.html* Guide to various sources of online news and tips for mining them.

- **Newspaper Archives on the Web:** *http://metalab.unc.edu/slanews/internet/archives.html* Compiled by the Special Libraries Association, News Division members, this state-by-state and country-by-country listing of news Web sites with archives gives State, City, link to Newspaper, link to archive portion of the newspaper, date the archive started, and information about the cost. Many of these archives require individual subscription to the news site, others are transactional purchases, pay as you go.

- **NewsTrawler:** *http://www.newstrawler.com* This interesting service is a sort of meta-search site for news archives. Plug in a search, select which papers to trawl and NewsTrawler goes and finds if there are any articles in the archive that match. Sort of cumbersome, but a really nice new application to ease the hopping around from news site to news site.

- **Speech and Transcript Center:** *http://gwis2.circ.gwu.edu/~gprice/speech.htm* Another awesome compilation by Gary Price, this one points you to places on the Web to find speeches from business leaders and government officials, transcripts of radio and television programs, Congressional hearings, and various government agencies.

Exercise

- Do a search on "antidisestablishmentarianism" in Northern Light (go to Special Collections by clicking on the "Power" tab along the top, then selecting "Special Collection" before entering and sending your search.) Do it again in Electric Library. What differences were there in the search results? (And if you didn't get anything – check your spelling!)
- Someone told you there was a great debate on "Meet the Press" last weekend. Find the transcript.
- Some kids at the local middle school got sick from something they ate in the cafeteria. You remember that happening a few years back to some school kids in Detroit, bad strawberries or something. See if you can find some background articles.

BOOKS AND DIRECTORIES

Some of the most useful reference books are available in database form, and, in that form, are even more useful. Because every word in a database is indexed, information that is hidden or difficult to find using a traditional book index is revealed in a database search. Many of these useful reference works are also available on *CD-ROM,* a particularly cost-effective method for searching frequently used books.

Now that some of the best and most basic reference books are available on the Web, every reporter's desktop is a library.

Many of the publishers who made their directories and reference books available through a commercial database service now provide access through their own Web site. A good example of this is the Gale Group. While their excellent resources, like the Encyclopedia of Associations and the Biography Master Index, are still available on Dialog: *http://www.dialog.com*, you can also go to the Gale Group Web site: *http://www.gale.com* and, if you have an account, search all their publications. Both are browser-based searches but one is through a vendor, the other through the publisher.

These kinds of shifts and options in the availability of basic resources make savvy shopping for information even more challenging.

Examples of book and directory databases

- **American Business Directory:** Information on over 10 million U.S. businesses with information from press releases, annual reports and other records.

- **Encyclopedia of Associations:** Over 440,000 nonprofit membership organizations worldwide are profiled.

- **Complete works of Shakespeare**

- **Books in Print:** Information on books currently in print from U.S. publishers.

- **Marquis Who's Who:** Detailed biographies of over 82,000 individuals.

- **Martindale-Hubble:** Legal directory.

- **Research Centers and Services Directory:** Information on almost 30,000 organizations conducting research worldwide.

- **Thomas Register:** Information on what is made, where it is made, and who makes it. Covers more than 180,000 U.S. and Canadian companies.

Uses in news research

- **Locate specific information:** Directory and reference book databases can help you track down people, quotes, companies, and obscure facts with only the sketchiest of information.

- **Find experts/sources:** Associations, foundations and research centers are good places to contact experts in specific topics.

- **Get ideas about the scope of a topic:** Sometimes just browsing through names of associations, research centers can give you angles to a story.

- **Background and reality check:** Don't rely on what someone tells you; use a directory to find other sources who can verify their statements or fill in holes in their information.

- **Get "fun facts" and color:** Backgrounding something that happened on a certain date, what else happened on that date? Describing how big something is – what else is that big? Finding trivia and colorful details can add flavor to your story.

Advantages of Book and Directory Databases

- Full text indexing allows hidden information to be easily located.

- These are often databases of expensive reference books, it may be cheaper to search as needed than it is to buy the book.

- The database version is usually updated with new information and corrections more quickly than the print version.

- Since these are from well-organized reference sources, the information is usually well edited and the information is reliable.

Disadvantages and cautions

- These are not necessarily comprehensive: Don't assume something does not exist just because it isn't found in a search.

■ Some of the information in directories is from submission by the company or person (American Business Directory, Who's Who) so you must not assume that the information given is the unvarnished truth. Always consider the source of the information – in book and directory searches, and any other kinds of research.

■ The structure of many of these databases is fairly rigid. In order to do searches on particular fields or elements, you must understand how the database is compiled. Some fields require use of specific terms or else you will not get valid results. Use the sheets provided by the database vendor detailing the structure of individual files.

■ Be careful when using Web-based reference books. Many of them are versions which are now in the public domain, but are extremely dated. Roget's Thesaurus, for example, is on the Web at: *http://humanities. uchicago.edu/forms_unrest/ROGET.html* but it's the 1911 version. Obviously, this would be of little use in tracking contemporary terms.

■ Some full-text versions of books on the Web have search functions so you can look for a term. Others are just the full text on the screen, a long, long, long, scroll of text. For those, use your *Edit/Find in Page* function on your browser to look for a word in the text.

Further cautions when looking at ready-reference books online:

■ **What is the source of the reference?** Is the reference an online version of a reputable reference source or is it a compilation by a hobbyist?

■ **When was the reference last updated?** How current is the online version, is there a more current print version, is there a more current version online somewhere else?

■ **Can you get to it?** Some libraries are making reference works available on the Internet, but may have copyright or license restrictions that allow only local or approved users access to the reference. Don't be frustrated by finding a great title in a search, but being denied access to the resource.

■ **How easy is it to get to?** If the connection to get to the Webster's dictionary is unreliable or slow and you use that dictionary all the time, it might be smarter to invest in a pulp-based version of the reference book! Time is money, spend it well.

■ **How easy is it to search?** Are you not finding information that you just know must be there? Be skeptical about the reliability of the search engine, ask questions of the resource provider to make sure you are using the resource properly.

■ **If it's not on the Internet that doesn't mean it doesn't exist:** Repeat after me, all the knowledge of the world is NOT on the Internet, all the knowledge of the world is NOT on the Internet. Don't think that if you can't find it on the Web there isn't anything on the topic. While Internet resources are growing quickly, there are billions of valuable reference books that are not, and probably will not, be available through Internet access. The Internet is a good source of supplementary information for some kinds of information searches. As valuable a resource as it is, it is not the be-all, end-all information tool.

With those cautions understood, let's look at some examples of books and ready reference sources on the Internet.

Services with book and directory databases

Commercial Services

- Dialog
- Nexis/Lexis
- *Congressional Quarterly*'s Washington Alert

On the Web

- **Internet Public Library: Reference Center:** *http://www.ipl. org/ref/* Subject and type of reference-organized links to great, reliable ready reference resources. Find almanacs, biographies, calculators, calendars, dictionaries, encyclopedias, quotes, etc. All these resources are free.

- **Research It!:** *http://www.iTools.COM/research-it/* This handy search site provides search boxes to dictionaries, thesauri, translators, quotation finders, biographical directories, geographical tools, currency calculators, and postal information. Love it!

- **Electric Library:** *http://www.elibrary.com* Frommer's travel guides, subject dictionaries, the Bible, the World Almanac, and the World Fact book are just a few of the hundreds of books and reports searchable in E-Library's book databases. You can do a free trial of the database.

- **Project Gutenberg:** *http://www.promo.net/pg/* PG has been making electronic versions of classic books available for the past 25 years. Light literature (*Alice in Wonderland*), heavy literature (the *Bible*), and reference works (*Webster's Unabridged Dictionary*) are available books. Find a title you want, download it to your computer and run your own searches on them.

- **The On-line Book Page:** *http://www.cs.cmu.edu/books.html* More than 9,000 books and 25,000 items of sheet music and archives are linked from this page. A great compilation service.

- **Web of Online Dictionaries:** *http://www.facstaff.bucknell.edu/ rbeard/diction.html* Hundreds of different dictionaries.

Exercises

- The flowery speaking Speaker of the House, in a confrontation with a opponent on a bill said, "Just as the King in *Love's Labour's Lost,* 'Now step I forth to whip hypocrisy'". You want to check if it really was the King in Shakespeare's play who said this.

- The seabird rescue mission director said, "If the pelican is worthy enough to be mentioned in the Bible, I think it is worthy enough to be protected…" Is the pelican mentioned in the Bible? Is it mentioned in every version of the Bible? Is the eagle mentioned? What about the robin? (Use this Bible browser…it has a great search template: *http://goon.stg.brown.edu/ bible_browser/pbeasy.shtml)*

- You're fighting with your editor about using the term "disintermediation" in a story about a financier's activities back in the early '70s. He said that term wasn't even in use back then (and he sort of wants you to explain to him what exactly it means). Prove that the term was in use and find a definition.

- You're the government affairs columnist and decide to write your next column in rhyme. Find some good words that rhyme with "democratic".

GOVERNMENT DOCUMENTS

Access to government publications used to be one of the big selling points of commercial database access. The ability to quickly look up and retrieve presidential speeches, texts of legislation and campaign contribution records was a tremendous aid to reporters. It came, however, at a cost, causing a great deal of controversy over the need to pay to retrieve government information that your tax dollars helped collect.

The impact of the World Wide Web and it's increasing use by government agencies to make official documents available is still being gauged by commercial database vendors. There had been attempts by the information industry lobby to close off the free access to some public documents (notably EDGAR, the electronic version of SEC documents) but they were unsuccessful and the number of government documents available on the Internet grows.

See more about the information made available by Government Agencies in Chapter 3: WWW Contents.

Advantages and Disadvantages of Use

While the disadvantage of a higher cost to access might weigh against the commercial vendor of government documents, there are some advantages to their use:

■ **Information dates back further:** Presidential speeches are available for free on the White House Web site: *http://www.whitehouse.gov/* but only dates back to 1993. Presidential Documents database on Nexis dates back to 1981, and on Westlaw to 1936.

■ **Accumulation of records:** Reports and studies sponsored by individual agencies may be sitting on their free Web site but you may have to go to a number of sites to do a search. Commercial database services can access compilations of these individual files, such as Dialog's access to National Technical Information Services' Bibliographic database. There are some government-specific search services available on the Web now.

- ■ **GovBot:** *http://ciir2.cs.umass.edu/Govbot/* More than 1,000,000 Web pages from Government and Military sites – free.
- ■ **Gov.Search:** *http://standard.northernlight.com/cgi-bin/govsearch_login.p/* Search more than 5,400 full text sources and the National Technical Information Service archive – there's a fee.
- ■ **FedStats:** *http://www.fedstats.gov/* Find statistics from more than 70 government agencies – free.

■ **More targeted searching:** Commercial services take advantage of elaborate record structures to allow for field searching which can help target the documents you need. Documents available on free services often do not have field searching capabilities.

■ **Faster:** Time is money, and sometimes connecting to those popular, free government databases on the Internet can be time costly exercises. The Census site: *http://www.census.gov* is often very slow to get into. When you need the information and you need it now, sometimes going to a commercial service is more efficient.

SOURCES

BOOKS

Government Information on the Internet, 2nd Ed., by Greg Notess. Bernan Associates, 1998

How to Access the Federal Government on the Internet 1998, by Bruce Maxwell. Congressional Quarterly, 1997.

Government on the Net, by James Evans. Nolo Press, 1998.

Keep in mind the disadvantages, too

■ **Tracking down source documents:** Often, the information you retrieve is a reference to a government document, which you then have to locate to get the full text. This is particularly true for older documents.

■ **Interpretation of data:** Statistics can be difficult to interpret; it is essential that you understand where the statistics come from and what they are based on, and use care as you compare statistics from one year to the next to be sure you are comparing like values.

Examples of Government Document Databases

■ CENDATA: Bureau of Census Reports
■ Department of State Bulletins
■ Security and Exchange Commission Reports
■ Patent Abstracts
■ Presidential Documents

Uses in news research

■ **Find facts, statistics:** The U.S. government collects data and statistics on virtually every topic. These databases help make those figures accessible. You can even do searches on a figure (say, the national debt) and see if there are other items with that number that come up which might make an interesting comparison.

■ **Reality check:** The capture of essentially every public word spoken by government officials, legislators, and executives means you can easily check back on what they've said in the past when you want to verify something they're saying now.

■ **Background:** Financial information, Congressional testimony, and other information can be used to help background people and companies you are writing about.

■ **Finding experts:** Check in the transcripts of Congress to find names of people who have appeared as experts and testified.

Services with Government Documents

■ Dialog
■ Dow Jones
■ Nexis/Lexis
■ Washington Alert
■ Westlaw

On the Web

■ U.S. Federal Government Agencies on the Web: *http://www.lib.lsu.edu/gov/fedgov.html*

■ State and Local Government on the Net: *http://www.piperinfo.com/state/states.html*

■ Governments on the World Wide Web: *http://www.gksoft.com/govt/en/us.html* – more than 12,000 entries from 219 countries

■ Political Resources on the Net: *http://www.agora.stm.it/politic/*

■ National Association of State Information Resource Executives: *http://www.nasire.org/statesearch*

- GPO Access on the Web: *http://gpo.sailor.lib.md.us* 100 govt. document databases to search.

Exercises

- How much has been allocated in the 1999 Federal Budget for Special Education programs? (Budget search available from GPO.)

- Find the Environmental Profile for your county (use the zip code search at the EPA site).

- Use Fedstats to find if there are any statistics about the "Brain Drain" of Foreign Doctoral Students staying in the U.S.

PEOPLE FINDERS / PUBLIC RECORDS DATABASES

Computer access to information about people is probably the most useful and most controversial area of computer-assisted research in newsrooms. These databases, from the simplest telephone look-up to more sophisticated dossier services, are invaluable to both deadline reporting and long term investigations.

Information about people comes from two sources: records gathered by government agencies and those gathered by business. Think of them as records of one's life as a citizen and records of one's life as a consumer.

Public records from government agencies have always been available, but in paper form they were difficult or time-consuming to access. Information about consumers is a new area, and probably the cause of most of the concerns about privacy. Each of these types of records has tremendous value in news research but requires extra care and knowledge when used.

Public Records Databases

Over the past decade many state and local government agencies have been moving towards electronic access to their records. While some of it may be useful in issues stories (i.e., statistics on health care or water quality or road characteristics), we'll be talking here about databases that can help you track down people, their associates, their assets and their personal histories.

The types of records, what they can provide, and what information you usually need to search by can help you determine what might help you get what you need. Some are statewide databases, others are local compilations, for which you would have to search county-by-county to get full coverage.

Useful Public Records Types

- **Motor vehicle information:** automobile registrations, driver's licenses, accident reports
    - **Can provide:** address, date of birth, driver history, social security number (in some states), physical characteristics of the driver (height, weight, race, sex, need for eyeglasses), type of automobile driven (make, model, year).
    - **Need to search by:** name (sometimes full name is required – sometimes date of birth is also required), driver's license number, VIN (vehicle identification number) or motor vehicle registration number.
- **Secretary of State filings:** incorporation records, uniform commercial code filing, limited partnerships

- **Can provide:** address information, names of business associates and associated businesses, name of company registered agent, address of the business, status of the business, names of debtors and creditors.
- **Need to search by:** name of officer or business name.

- **Property records:** tax appraisals and mortgage filings
  - **Can provide:** name and address of owner, characteristics of the house (sq. ft., no. of rooms), mortgage holder and amount, appraised value, who sold the house and when.
  - **Need to search by:** address of the property, owner or seller's name.

- **Utility records:** water and sewer billings
  - **Can provide:** name and address of owner (useful for rented properties), delinquency of payment. (Check your water board members and see how they are doing with their bills!)
  - **Need to search by:** property address, owner's name.

- **Voter registration records**
  - **Can provide:** address information, party affiliation, last election they voted.
  - **Need to search by:** name.

- **Marriage/divorce records**
  - **Can provide:** maiden name of bride, dates of marriage – divorce, whether there were previous marriages.
  - **Need to search by:** name.

- **Occupational licenses**
  - **Can provide:** information about business line, address.
  - **Need to search by:** name.

- **Civil and criminal court cases/criminal history**
  - **Can provide:** plaintiff and defendant names, lawyers' names, case file numbers (to get the full case record), arrest records.
  - **Need to search by:** name, case number.

- **Other records of interest:** concealed weapons permits, boat and aircraft registrations, bankruptcy filings, mortgage default records, aircraft ownership, statewide criminal records.

Ways Agencies Make Their Databases Available Online

In addition to the regular telephone and mail-in request fulfillment services most government agencies have, many have been making public records available online through a variety of means.

DIRECT ACCESS TO THE AGENCY'S COMPUTER: i.e., Minnesota's dial-in account to Department of Motor Vehicle records.

- **Advantages:** The data is as current as the agency has available, you are searching the same database they use.

- **Disadvantages:** Sometimes the search interface is not designed for consumer use, but for agency use, and is not very user friendly. It is possible the agency can monitor what is being searched on the database. Sometimes the database is available only during regular office hours.

AGENCY SELLS DATABASE TO A VENDOR: This is the fastest growing area, public records resellers buy and repackage public records databases.

- **Advantages:** The searching and look of the database is more consumer oriented and usually easier to use. There is often a wide range of databases available (by type of record or geographic area) providing "one-stop shopping" for public records. Some services pull records together, giving you a dossier of the person you are looking for. Usually, there is a virtually 24-hour, seven day a week access to the records.

■ **Disadvantages:** Records are often not as current as direct access to the agency's database, be sure you know when the records are updated. All counties in a state database may not be represented, be sure you know the coverage of the data. You are paying a premium for the access and searchability of the data, it may be the more expensive access option.

THROUGH A BULLETIN BOARD SERVICE (BBS): Federal circuit courts and bankruptcy courts offer bbs dial-in service, called PACER, to appellate court decisions and docket information. There is a central registration number to call (800-676-6856). Click to the Directory of Electronic Access to U.S. Federal Courts for more information: *http://www.uscourts. gov/PubAccess.html*

■ **Advantages:** Fairly inexpensive ($.60/minute), some districts are free. Does not require high-end computer to access.

■ **Disadvantages:** Separate access to the different courts, no centralized call-in. Different courts have their bbs arranged differently.

RECORDS SEARCH ON THE WEB: As with every other kind of information, everyone is migrating to the Web. Some of the PACER-accessed courts' records are now searchable on Web sites. You can find a list at the Web address above.

Some state, county and local agencies are making searches of their records available on the Web. In mid-'99, 24 states and 163 local counties or cities were making some records searchable.

Others are providing access to public records for free. The University of Kentucky has put the state's Dept. of Health Statistics files on their Web site: *http://ukcc.uky.edu/~vitalrec/* Search for death records (1911-1992), marriage records (1973-1993), and divorces (1973-1993).

■ **Advantages:** FREE! Quick and easy search template. Provides basic information (age, race, residence county, and date of event).

■ **Disadvantages:** The search is by name only.

Where to find free Public Records

■ **Free Public Records Sites:** *http://www.brbpub.com/pubrecsites. htm* This handy listing is from BRB, the public records directory people.

■ **Public Records Database Listing:** *http://www.pac-info.com* Over 900 free state public records databases.

LOCATOR SERVICE SUBSCRIBES TO VARIOUS VENDORS: Many service companies are springing up that subscribe to the various public records databases and offer comprehensive search and retrieval of records in both electronic and paper form. Most of these services have a Web site.

■ **Advantages:** You don't have to have subscriptions to a number of different services. They can access records in a number of forms through network of searchers in various cities.

■ **Disadvantages:** Probably the most costly option since the search service passes along the cost of the search as well as a service charge. Usually, quick turnaround service costs extra, may be several days delay in getting some records.

Examples of vendors of Public Records on the Web

This is by no means an endorsement of these particular services, they just provide an interesting inventory of the types of records available.

- DataQuest: *http://www.nmia.com/~search/dataques.html*
- Sherlock: *http://www.ameri.com/sherlock/sherlock.htm*
- 1800 US search: *http://www.1800ussearch.com*
- Aaron's Private Investigations: *http://www.aaronspi.com/*

Find Public Records Services

- Search for Online Search Firms/Distributors/Gateways: *http://www.publicrecordsources.com/* Another great resource from BRB Publications.

PURCHASE TAPES OF THE DATA AND ACCESS ON YOUR OWN COMPUTER: i.e., Waterbury, CT's city employees database has been purchased and stored on city reporters' laptop computers, allowing quick checks of names, addresses, salaries of employees.

- **Advantages:** No cost for searching after the data has been purchased. The data can run on software that is designed for easy use.

- **Disadvantages:** For databases with frequent updates and changes, the purchased database is quickly outdated.

HOW TO LOCATE PUBLIC RECORDS DATABASES

Not all states or local governments offer the same level of access to similar records. Not all records of the same type have the same information from state to state (for example, New York does not require the listing of officers names in the corporate filings). Although, on the state level, some public records search companies are getting more comprehensive access to records, the compilation of local level records is still far away. Here are some ways you can track down public records for your state, and local area:

- **Check with the agency itself:** Determine which agencies' files you would find useful for routine checks (corporate filings, drivers' records and property records are generally the most useful). Call the agency's data manager and see whether you can arrange for direct access or even the purchase of files to load on your own computer.

- **Check with public records database vendors:** Several database vendors specialize in public records access. Shop around the different services to see which ones have the types of records you want and the most comprehensive coverage. (See the list of vendors below.)

- **Check with your state press association:** The press association should be tracking public records access in your state. Several states have developed guides to public records.

- **Check with a university data center:** Many large universities have data centers with tape libraries of state data. They can tell you the status on availability of different types of records.

- **Check with the state information center or the city/county data processing office:** These are the keepers of the information inventory. They will know what databases are available and the access there is to the records.

- **Do a Web search:** Genealogists are using the Web as a way to share information about how to track down records about people. Do a search in one of the search sites for "birth certificates" or "death records" and you'll get all kinds of listings of places to call. Many will require some turn-around time, so don't think you can do this on deadline!

   - Check out: USGenWeb Archives: "Building a Virtual Courthouse" *http://www.rootsWeb.com/~usgenweb/*
   - Look at Vital Records Information: *http://www.vitalrec.com* for a listing by state of where to get birth, death, marriage and divorce records.

A critical step in locating public records is knowing your rights for access to the records. Again, your state press association: *http://newspapers.com/npcom8.htm* or the Reporter's Committee for Freedom of the Press: *http://www.rcfp.org/* are good sources for information about records access.

Consumer Records Databases

Every time you change your address, subscribe to a magazine, get a telephone number, or apply for a credit card, you leave an electronic trail. So do the people you are looking for when you are reporting the news. Database vendors offer access to some of these databases which can be very useful in tracking down people or providing key pieces of biographical information. The access to records of different types can also help you verify, from a couple of different sources, information you have found.

In the past couple of years, information that had previously been available to researchers has been removed. For example, information from credit headers used to tell where the person worked. This is no longer available, except to those with permissible (under the Fair Credit Reporting Act: *http://www.ftc.gov/os/statutes/fcrajump.htm*) use of credit information (reporters are not a category of "fair users"!).

But there are still useful compilations of data from consumer based records such as:

■ **Post Office Change of Address:** This had previously been widely available, now it is accessible on only a few services (WDIA's National Credit Information Network, for one). This has the change of address forms people fill out to have their mail forwarded to a new address.

■ **People Finders:** With just a person's name and the state he or she lives in, you can get a record giving address and telephone number. These databases are usually compiled from standard directories (such as telephone books) and other sources such as product response cards and magazine subscription cards.

■ **Address Search:** Nationwide criss-cross directories allow you to search on an address and get information on who lives there, telephone number, age (sometimes), and other residents. These usually have a feature allowing you to see the names of neighbors with their telephone numbers and addresses. A recent example of the usefulness of neighbor access. When a plane crashed in North Carolina, an Associated Press reporter had the address of the church near the crash site. He looked up the address, got neighbors listings and started calling. The second number reached a woman who had had a burned survivor of the crash stumble onto her front porch just minutes earlier.

- **Phone Search:** A compilation of listed telephone numbers. There are a number of phone search products and services. Be careful to determine which is the most current, most frequently updated and which might include unlisted numbers. (Unlisted numbers would be in there if someone put it on another source which is used in compiling the record – magazine subscription form or credit application, for example. You won't get unlisted numbers from the telephone company.)

- **Credit Headers:** A database of information extracted from credit reports. It does not include specific financial information but can provide you with current and previous addresses, social security number, month and year of birth, spouse's name.

Cautions to Use of Public Records and Consumer Records

As useful as these databases are in locating people you need to talk to, they are also the riskiest to use and potentially the most expensive. Keep these guidelines in mind:

- **Verify, verify, verify:** The old computer adage, "Garbage In, Garbage Out," was never truer than with these databases. Usually this information is contributed by the person it is about (is anyone honest about their weight on driver's licenses?), comes from handwritten forms which are keypunched into the database. Errors are rampant and it is essential that any information you find from these files be verified.

- **Consider the source:** Understand how the data came to be in the database, what is required of that particular record, what kind of checking is done of the veracity of the information. Public records databases may be more reliable than consumer records, but someone with no car, property records or utility bills may be found in consumer records.

- **Get specifics:** If you only have the person's name you need to search, and it is a common name, you might as well not search. Unless you have some specific information that can identify the entry as the person you are looking for, you cannot assume you have found the right person.

- **Don't expect miracles:** Some data is just not available. You can check the same name in different databases and just get the same information over and over. Know what you are searching. Also, privacy laws are getting stricter, know what you can reasonably expect to find, and don't expect more.

- **Shop carefully:** Know what you are paying for and which database is being searched when you look at different vendors. You may be charged a premium for searching a database you could have gotten at directly for much cheaper.

- **Don't forget the good old paper trail:** Lots of information is still not online. Much of the information that is online is just a reference to the full file which you'll need to get from the agency which created it. These sources are often a good pointer to places to check although they are not the whole picture. Remember, it's called Computer-Assisted Research, not Computer-Completed Research.

Where to find consumer records information

For a comparison of the major vendors of public records, who also usually have consumer-based records searches, too, see below.

On the Web there are lots of people-finder services with telephone and address look-up available. Which one is the best? Well, the one that has the name you are looking for in it! But that will be different for different people.

Someone from New York asked me which service I preferred and I ran his name and my name through a few of the services to show the difference in results:

Anywho: *http://www.anywho.com* Had him, didn't have me

WhoWhere: *http://www.whowhere.com* Didn't have either of us

Yahoo! People: *http://people.yahoo.com* Had us both

Switchboard: *http://www.switchboard.com* Had me, didn't have him

As with all the search services, get to know a few well, but know where the others are in case your regular route of searching doesn't get you where you need to go.

How to find People Finder Sites

■ Telephone Directories on the Web: *http://www.teldir.com* The Internet's original and most detailed index of online phone books.

■ PeopleSearch: *http://peoplesearch.net* A meta-search site 10 different people-finder databases. Each search will spawn a new browser window – to quickly close browser windows, click ALT-F4.

■ Duff Wilson's Reporter's Desktop: *http://www.reporter.org/desktop* Duff, a reporter at the *Seattle Times*, has put together a handy telephone and address search section.

■ Internet Prospector: People: *http://w3.uwyo.edu/~prospect/bio.html* Great tips on people finding.

Exercises

■ An accused bigamist named Charlie McGillis admits he married one woman in Colorado in the early '80s but he says he divorced her there a few years later. Find the marriage record and see if there was a divorce.

■ An old colleague of yours, Steve Doig, has just come up in conversation and you decide to get in touch. Find him (he supposedly quit reporting to go be a professor somewhere).

■ Find Kurt Cobain's social security number (his death index record would have it.)

Web sites

BRB Publications: *http://www.brbpub.com* 888-299-7172

BRB publishes a series of invaluable handbooks on public records access including: *Sourcebook of Public Record Providers, Sourcebook of County Court Records, Sourcebook of State Public Records.* Their publication, *Public Records Online* ($19.95), includes dial-up government systems, Web sites of substance and private industry databases. BRB also publishes the *1999 MVR Book*, which helps you determine privacy restrictions and access procedures for motor vehicle and driver history records.

Public and Consumer Records Vendors

CDB Infotek: *http://www.cdb.com* 888-333-3365

Database Technologies/Autotrack: *http://www.dbt.com* 800-279-7710

Information America: *http://www.infoam.com* 800-235-4008

IRSC: *http://www.irsc.com* 800-640-4772

Know-X: *http://www.knowx.com* 800-235-4008

FOR FURTHER INFORMATION ABOUT PUBLIC RECORDS AND PEOPLE FINDING:

Get the Facts on Anyone, 3rd edition. By Dennis King. Arco Pub., 1999. $14.95
  Chapters include: Basic Concepts, Basic Tools, Basic Techniques, Finding Missing People, Backgrounding the Individual, Court Records...

You, Too, Can Find Anyone, by Joseph Culligan. FJA Inc., 1998. $19.95.

The Reporter's Handbook, 3rd edition. Edited by John Ullmann and Steve Weinberg. St. Martin's Press, New York, 1996.
  Subtitled *An Investigator's Guide to Documents and Techniques.* This is the handbook for tracking records, both electronic and paper. A new edition is coming soon.

Naked in Cyberspace: How to Find Personal Information Online, by Carole A. Lane. Cyberage Books, 1996 (new edition to come).

Lexis-Nexis: *http://www.lexis-nexis.com* 800-227-9597

WDIA: *http://www.wdia.com/dunhome.htm* – many records are searched offline. Has access to credit header information, a good source of addresses.

COMPARISON OF VENDORS' CONTENTS AND COST FOR VARIOUS RECORDS (compiled by Kitty Bennett, *St. Petersburg Times* – March 1999)

Startup/Monthly/Other Charges

- **CDB Infotek:** $0 / $25
- **Database Technologies:** $0 / $25 – waived if monthly charges exceed $100. $1.75 / minute for Autotrack, set fees for each record search for Autotrack XP (Web version)
- **Information America:** $50 / $55 / $.69 min. connect time, $.02 per line printed
- **Know-X:** $0 / $0 / $.50 peak time charge from 11 am - 6 pm EST for most searches
- **IRSC:** $150 / $30
- **Lexis-Nexis:** $0 / $25 - $125 monthly administration fee
- Free or cheap alternatives: check list of public records databases at http://www.pac-info.com

Aircraft Ownership (by name) – National

■ CDB Infotek:	$20
■ Database Technologies:	$5 (approx.)
■ Information America:	$25
■ Know-X:	$16.50
■ IRSC:	$15
■ Lexis-Nexis:	$41
■ Free or cheap alternatives:	Landings: *http://www.landings.com*

Aircraft Ownership (by N-number) – National

■ CDB Infotek:	N/A
■ Database Technologies:	$5 (approx.)
■ Information America:	N/A
■ Know-X:	N/A
■ IRSC:	$15
■ Lexis-Nexis:	$41
■ Free or cheap alternatives:	Landings: *http://www.landings.com*

Corporate Records

■ CDB Infotek:	$16 (46 states)
■ Database Technologies:	$9 (approx.) (43 states)
■ Information America:	$75 (46 states)
■ Know-X:	$16.50 (46 states)
■ IRSC:	$16 per state (7 states)
■ Lexis-Nexis:	$87 (45 states)

- Free or cheap alternatives: Locating U.S. Corporation
    Records Online
    http://w3.uwyo.edu/~prospect/
    secstate.html

Social Security Death Index – National

- CDB Infotek: $20
- Database Technologies: $5 (approx.)
- Information America: $25
- Know-X: $6
- IRSC: $9
- Lexis-Nexis: $41
- Free or cheap alternatives: *http://www.ancestry.com/ssdi/*
    advanced.htm

Statewide Criminal Search (per state)

- CDB Infotek: N/A
- Database Technologies: $17.50 – $47 + $7 per name
    (22 states)
- Information America: N/A
- Know-X: N/A
- IRSC: $16
- Lexis-Nexis: N/A
- Free or cheap alternatives: TX criminal convictions:
    http://records.txdps.state.tx.us

Motor Vehicle Ownership (per state)

- CDB Infotek: $8 - $25
- Database Technologies: $5 - $17 for all states (32 states)
- Information America: $25 (TX only)
- Know-X: N/A
- IRSC: $5 per state + various state fees
    (43 states)
- Lexis-Nexis: $41 - $51 per state (5 states)

Driving History (per state)

- CDB Infotek: $4.95 - $23 (46 states)
- Database Technologies: $3.10 - $21.20 + $7 per name
    (22 states)
- Information America: N/A
- Know-X: N/A
- IRSC: $5 per state + various state fees
    (50 states)
- Lexis-Nexis: N/A

Property Record

- CDB Infotek: $15 (43 states, 692 counties)
- Database Technologies: $5 - $25 (45 states, 786 counties)
- Information America: $75 (38 states, 528 counties)
- Know-X: $16.50 (38 states, 528 counties)

- IRSC: $20 per state (43 states, 613 counties)
- Lexis-Nexis: $120 (49 states, 976 counties)
- Free or cheap alternatives: *http://www.brbpub.com/ pubrecsites.htm* or check individual county home pages

Bankruptcy – National

- CDB Infotek: $5 (52 states)
- Database Technologies: $12 (51 states)
- Information America: $90 (53 states)
- Know-X: $20 (53 states)
- IRSC: $7.75 (50 states)
- Lexis-Nexis: $150 (51 states)
- Free or cheap alternatives: Pacer (800-676-6856 to register) *http://www.uscourts.gov/ PubAccess.html* Checking 1 name costs about $3.00

Professional License

- CDB Infotek: $17 per state (10 states)
- Database Technologies: $9 (47 states)
- Information America: $75 (20 states)
- Know-X: $16.50 (20 states)
- IRSC: $17 per state (50 states)
- Lexis-Nexis: $87 (14 states)
- Free or cheap alternatives: Natl Assoc of State Info. Resource Executives *http://www.nasire.org/ stateSearch/displayCategory.cfm? Category=regulation*

Civil Records (lawsuits, etc.)

- CDB Infotek: $7.75–$50 (4 states, 31 counties)
- Database Technologies: $32–$72 + $7/name (11 states, 26 counties)
- Information America: $90 for all states (45 states, 505 counties)
- Know-X: $26.50 for all states (45 states, 505 counties)
- IRSC: $8 (3 states)
- Lexis-Nexis: $87 for all states (4 states, 21 counties)
- Free or cheap alternatives: *http://www.brbpub.com/ pubrecsites.htm* or check individual county home pages

Comparison of Property Records by state and the number of counties, parishes or cities covered in each service. Numbers in italics indicate that the whole state is covered. This list was compiled by Kitty Bennett in March 1999.

State	CDB Infotek	DBT (AutoTrack)	Information America/Know-X	IRSC	Lexis-Nexis
Alabama	9	10	9	9	10
Alaska	1	4	0	1	5
Arizona	*15*	*15*	*15*	*15*	*15*
Arkansas	4	2	0	4	4
California	*58*	*58*	*58*	0	*58*
Colorado	13	13	11	14	14
Connecticut	15	0	0	9*	8
Delaware	2	1	1	1	*3*
DC	*1*	*1*	*1*	*1*	*1*
Florida	*67*	*67*	*67*	66	*67*
Georgia	21	21	15	21	55
Hawaii	*4*	*4*	*4*	*4*	*4*
Idaho	0	2	0	1	2
Illinois	21	11	6	16	16
Indiana	0	3	0	0	6
Iowa	1	5	1	1	7
Kansas	2	0	1	2	2
Kentucky	4	1	1	4	2
Louisiana	1	6	1	2	7
Maine	0	0	0	0	0
Maryland	*24*	*24*	*24*	*24*	*24*
Massachusetts	11*	*14*	10	11*	*14*
Michigan	6	7	2	5	15
Minnesota	8	12	8	8	13
Mississippi	1	3	1	1	8
Missouri	4	7	3	4	9
Montana	0	37	0	0	56
Nebraska	1	2	0	1	2
Nevada	4	4	3	4	4
New Jersey	*21*	*21*	*21*	*21*	*21*
New Mexico	2	4	2	2	6
New York	*62*	60	59	61	*62*
N. Carolina	14	22	8	14	25
N. Dakota	0	1	0	0	1
Ohio	29	27	12	32	40
Oklahoma	10	8	10	10	12
Oregon	10	11	6	10	12

Pennsylvania	19	28	15	16	33
Rhode Island	1	0	0	1*	5
S. Carolina	14	12	8	14	15
Tennessee	95	95	95	95	95
Texas	23	39	16	25	52
U.S. Virgin Islands	0	3	3	0	3
Utah	4	4	4	4	4
Vermont	2	0	1	1*	14
Virginia	19	33	18	19	56
Washington	11	8	6	9	10
W. Virginia	55	55	0	55	55
Wisconsin	14	19	2	17	22
Wyoming	0	2	0	0	2
TOTAL	**692**	**786**	**528**	**613**	**976**

*In some states, IRSC and CDB have records for cities, rather than those for counties or independent cities.

Where there were several cities in one county, they were counted as a single county

If these two charts don't convince you of the need to do some comparison shopping, in terms of pricing and coverage, I don't know what will!

Comparisons of the Major Commercial Services

DIALOG: *http://www.dialog.com*

Description

500 databases covering business, news, patents, trademarks, science and government. More than 100 U.S. papers. 221 unique files that don't appear anywhere else.

Startup/monthly and/or yearly charges

$295 / $75 monthly minimum, $144 annual membership fee

Telecommunications charges/minute

20 cents for most users

Time online

Free

Searching charges

Charges by "dialunit," which are units of usage of system "resources" when executing commands, typically $1-3 per search.

Per search in newspaper files

Retrieving 10 articles from newspaper files costs about $3 worth of dialunits.

Per newspaper article downloaded, printed or viewed

$2.60

Headlines viewed

Free

Sec 10k filings

$12.00

Frugality tips

Use "DialogWeb," one of several different Web-based flavors of Dialog. It's almost always cheaper than using other flavors, and doesn't require any knowledge of Dialog's command syntax. DialogWeb also allows you to do an initial search for "hits" for free

DOW JONES: *http://www.dj.com*

Description

80-million articles from 6,000 publications, plus market research, analyst reports and historical market data. Data can be output in a variety of formats, including spreadsheets.

Startup/monthly and/or yearly charges

$0 / $69 per password, per year

Telecommunications charges/minute

Free

Time online

Free

Searching charges

Free

Per search in newspaper files

Free

Per newspaper article downloaded, printed or viewed

$2.95

Headlines viewed

Free

Sec 10k filings

$5.95

Frugality tips

Do a search and check out the lead sentences, all for free, to see if you want a story before you pay for it. Consider other sources for the articles you want, such as free, Web-based archives.

LEXIS-NEXIS

Description

1.4-billion news stories, legal documents, financial and market reports, legislative materials and more from 22,000 sources arranged into nearly 10,000 databases. Adds 4.6-million documents a week.

Startup/monthly and/or yearly charges

$0 / $25-125 monthly administration fee

Telecommunications charges/minute

Free

Time online

Free

Searching charges

Encourages flat-rate pricing, which can range from $49 per week for "requester" (collection of 70 papers) to $10,000 per month and up. Flat-rate for public records databases is $4,200/mo. If not on flat-rate plan, a single search costs from $0 to $175.

Per search in newspaper files

$6 for a single publication, $36 for a group of nearly 1,000 newspapers, trade journals and wires

Per newspaper article downloaded, printed or viewed

$3.50 for most items, viewing free

Headlines viewed

Free

Sec 10k filings

$40 ($15 + $25 printing/downloading fee)

Frugality tips

Some really clever and frugal searchers have been known to start a search in the morning, save it (searches can be kept "live" til 2 a.m. the next day), and then "modify" it for free to get several searches for the price of one.

Profiles provided by Kitty Bennett.

Evaluating Information Online

When I send out surveys before training sessions I ask people to rank their main concerns when using the Internet. I want to know what they would like to get more comfortable with.

Almost everyone responds first with "I'd like to learn how to search better, I get too many results." But the one that comes in second is, "I'd like to know how to judge the information on the Internet. How can I tell whether or not the information I find is reliable?"

It used to make me somewhat puzzled that journalists, whose life's work is to scratch the surface of what they see and get down to the truth, were so flummoxed by the delivery of information on the Web. They are trained BS detectors. They know how to go behind the spin and find the reality. They can look at the documents and listen to the glib statements and then ask the questions that reveal the whats, whys and hows.

So, why are so many so stymied when they get in front of the computer screen? Why do they think the process of validation and verification of information on the Internet is any different than the one they employ everyday with sources, press releases, faxed documents or stuff sent in the mail?

In this section we'll step through a couple of different approaches to thinking about Internet-delivered information. One comes from a journalist, the other from some librarians – representatives of two groups who base the credibility of their own work on their ability to judge the credibility of the information they use.

But before we start a few words about information on the Internet.

- The Internet did not invent mis-information or disinformation.
- The Internet did not create rumormongering.
- The Internet did not spawn propaganda.
- The Internet is not responsible for dirty data and stupid statistics.

All of these have been around forever.

They just have a new distribution outlet. The Internet DOES make it possible for the mis-information, disinformation, rumormongering, dirty data and stupid statistics to be distributed more quickly and widely than in the past. That's the bad news. But the good news is that there are more people looking at what is distributed on the Web and who will provide the voice of reason (good examples are the rumor-control Web sites where hoaxes and urban myths are debunked).

Think about it this way. Can you trust what people say in a newsgroup or a chat room? Could you trust what you heard in a bar, or a man-on-the-street interview, a PTA meeting, or from fans in the stands? The answer, of course, is no. The old adage of "If your mother says she loves you, check it out," predates the Internet, but will serve you well here, too.

If you pull up a document on the Web and you can't tell where it came from, what would you do with it? Well, what would you do if you got a fax or a document in a manila envelope with no return address? Check it out.

If someone sends you e-mail and you don't know who they are, can you believe what they are telling you? If you get a phone call from someone you don't know, can you believe what they are telling you? It's your job to find

SOURCES

Web Wisdom: How to evaluate and create information quality on the Web, by Jan Alexander and Marsha Ann Tate. Lawrence Erlbaum, 1999.

Evaluating Quality on the Net, by Hope Tillman: *http://www.tiac.net/ users/hope/findqual.html*

Evaluating Web Resources: Bibliography. *http://www2.widener. edu/Wolfgram-Memorial-Library/webstrbib.htm*

ICYouSee: T is for Thinking *http://www.ithaca.edu/library/Training/ hott.html*
   A nice tutorial on Web evaluation.

Internet Detective: *http://sosig.ac.uk/desire/internet-detective.html*
   For a different approach to teaching critical thinking about Web sites.

out if you can believe what you read or hear no matter what medium is used to deliver it.

Those criteria you used in the past to check out the document in the manila envelope, the overheard conversation, or the phoned in tip will serve you well as you use the information you find on the Web.

Now, here are a couple of ways to think about the evaluation of information on the Web.

MIDIS

Steve Miller, *New York Times* assistant to the technology editor, came up with a hierarchical approach to judging Web site information. Modestly called MIDIS: the Miller Internet Data Integrity Scale, he has a four-level scale for information found on the Web and how comfortable a journalist can be in using it.

Most reliable to use are:

Government Data: Federal, State & Local

Miller says, "While you might personally question the data, you are safe in quoting from it ("…according to the National Transportation Safety Board…")."

Next are:

University Studies: Peer-reviewed, Sub-Doctoral

Miller says, "Most studies by recognized experts in a field are still reviewed by peers. Quoting from these studies is also a safe bet with attribution."

Following that are:

Special Interest Groups: an agenda doesn't mean the data is flawed

Miller says, "Even though we know that these groups have a political agenda, it does not follow that their data is flawed. It's also safe to use the data since it is attributable. ("A study by Amnesty International claims that….")

And the least reliable, on the MIDIS hierarchy are:

Other: Who is this person and why is he publishing this data?

Miller says: "This is information published on someone's homepage. Since anyone can put anything on a homepage it's a coin toss whether the data has any validity."

(Read a full description of Steve's MIDIS analysis at: *http://www. freedomforum.org/technology/1997/10/stevechart2.asp)*

AUTHORITY, ACCURACY, OBJECTIVITY, CURRENCY, COVERAGE

Journalists have the 5 Ws and the H (who, what, when, where, why, how) as a checklist of questions to answer when covering a story.

Librarians have the 2 As, 2 Cs and the O (authority, accuracy, objectivity, currency, coverage) as a checklist of questions to answer when evaluating information resources. The criteria that has been used to determine whether a book was a good one to add to a collection serves well when judging the validity of information found on the Web.

Two librarians at Widener University, Jan Alexander and Marsha Ann Tate, have created practical guides to evaluating information found on different kinds of Web sites. Their site, "Evaluating Web Resources":

http://www2.widener.edu/Wolfgram-Memorial-Library/webeval.htm, provides checklists for Web evaluation.

They have divided Web contents into five different Web page types:

- Advocacy
- Business/Marketing
- News
- Informational
- Personal

For each type, they list questions you should ask about the page you are looking at. They say "The greater number of questions listed below answered "yes", the more likely it is you can determine whether the source is of high information quality." They even have some that are in bold which, they say, if you cannot answer "yes," why would you even THINK about using the information!

Authority: Can you tell who put the page together? Is it an "official" site? Is there contact information for the people who put the page together? Can you tell who wrote the material on the page and what their qualifications are?

Accuracy: Do they give the source for any "factual" information on the page that you can independently verify? Is the page well-edited? (If they are shoddy with spelling and grammar, they may be shoddy with accuracy, too.)

Objectivity: Are biases clearly stated? Is advertising clearly differentiated from information content?

Currency: Can you tell when the page was written, posted to the Web, updated?

Coverage: Is it clear what the page intends to address? Does it cover those areas well or are important issues left out?

Their Web site, and a book, *WEB WISDOM: How to Evaluate and Create Information Quality on the Web* are worth spending some time with.

Exercises

Look over Alexander and Tate's Web evaluation criteria and then take a look at the following. Which of these sites would you use? Why would you or why would you not use them?

1.) You're looking for background on biological warfare:

http://www.brad.ac.uk/acad/sbtwc/

http://www.mvhs.srvusd.k12.ca.us/~cchu/bio/feature.html

http://www.calpoly.edu/~drjones/chemwarf.html

2.) An Islamic school is opening in your town and you need to know more about Islamic education traditions:

http://www.islamicedfoundation.com

http://home.ici.net/~taadah/taadah.html

http://www.islamicity.org/Education

3.) You're looking for information about arthritis:

http://www.arthritis.org

http://www.pfizer.com/chc/bengay/tac.htm

http://www.canoe.com/Health9902/17_arthritis.html

"Everyone gets so much information all day long that they lose their common sense."

Gertrude Stein

Bottom line, with good training, clear policies, helpful guides, and sensible procedures, the issues the newsroom might have with using the Internet should be resolved.

TRAINING ISSUES

It always amazes me that huge capital budgets rarely have a line in them for training. This has certainly been the case with the shift to desktop access to the Internet. There's money for the hardware and the software, but none for the wetware – the people who will be using it.

There are many approaches to providing training on the Internet. Much of your approach depends on the current state of Internet usage in your newsroom, your goals for usage by the newsroom, and the resources you have available for training.

There is a tiered approach that many newsrooms take.

Evangelism: Initially, you're trying to drum up interest and enthusiasm about the Internet. Have large group sessions with demos and talks by journalists from inside or outside the newsroom about how they have used the Internet in their work. Try to spread the word broadly about what the Internet is and how it can be useful, even essential, in reporting. The goal is to whet their appetite and get them to want to learn how to do it.

Technical: Hold training sessions on the "technical" aspects of Internet use (browser basics, how to use their e-mail system). These are often done in huge sweeps of the newsroom. The goal is to get everyone up to a certain level of functional knowledge of the Internet software.

Departmental: Many newsroom training approaches then try to customize the training on use of specific Internet and Web techniques around the work of particular desks. What does the business desk need to use on the Internet? What would help the copy editors? How can feature writers take advantage of the Web? One of the goals here is to get a few people in those departments to become the point persons that can help others in the department when they have questions.

Individual: Ideally, training is on-going and personalized. A 20-minute session focusing on what an individual's daily information tasks are and pointing them to some techniques and resources to accomplish them might be the most useful approach of all. It will give that extra boost that will get someone convinced of the Internet's usefulness to them and their work. It will give them the confidence to explore further.

Who should do the training? If you have a news research center, the information professionals in the department would be the ideal trainers. That is certainly part of their training, to facilitate the use of information by people who need it. As we move to end-user information environments, the role of the news library will move away from being the gatekeeper of the information to being a facilitator of its use and access.

If you don't have a news research center, designating a few Web-savvy (and enthusiastic) people in the newsroom can be a good approach. For the initial training stages, bringing in an outside consultant to provide mass training can be useful. But, ultimately you'll be best served by developing an in-house network of experts and enthusiasts who can routinely pollinate the newsroom with Internet ideas and support.

Read more about it

- "Training Helps *Courier-Post* Staff Navigate The Web", *http://www. gannett.com/go/newswatch/97/december/nw1224-3.htm*

Resources about training

NICAR: *http://www.nicar.org* NICAR (the National Institute for Computer Assisted Reporting) has an "on-the-road" training team which can organize a regional workshop or internal newsroom training. There are some great resources on their Web site for trainers.

Make great training materials in 30 minutes or less: *http://www.saturn. vcu.edu/~jcsouth/* Find this document, and lots of other great materials at Jeff South's site at Virginia Commonwealth University.

Poynter Institute: "Reporting with the Internet": *http://www.poynter. org/class/L404/1997/L404_work.htm* Training modules developed by participants of the Poynter Institute's "Reporting with the Internet" seminar, 1997.

http://www.poynter.org/class/L404/1998/L404_train.htm An explanation of the elements of a training plan design and links to some Internet training resources developed for the 1998 Poynter, "Reporting with the Internet" seminar.

Journalism Net: *http://www.journalismnet.com/* Canadian journalist Julian Sher has developed a resource page for journalists that includes a section on training resources (but check out the other things, too).

Library of Congress: Internet guides, tutorials, and training information: *http://lcweb.loc.gov/global/internet/training.html* A selective list of resources for trainers and for self-guided learning of the Web.

Net Learn: *http://www.rgu.ac.uk/~sim/research/netlearn/callist.htm* A compilation of well organized and annotated resources for learning and teaching the Web.

RESOURCE SHARING ISSUES

In the early days of the Web when people found a great site, they told someone else about it, maybe. Or they sometimes would exchange bookmark lists. But, for the most part, knowledge about good resources on the Web was held in little pockets all over the newsroom.

Then came the "intranet" – an internal site which uses the browser software and links to the Internet to make resources on the Web easy to catalog, organize and search. In many newsrooms, the news library took the lead on developing these intranets. They quickly grew to include not just glorified bookmark lists, but links to manuals and training guides, internal databases of information (personnel directories), access to acquired databases from outside agencies, information helpful to employees of the organization.

Danish Broadcasting Corporation News Research manager Thomas Hedin created an intranet for his newsroom. "We have started with introducing our intranet to the TV-news journalists. Most of them look like they have seen the face of God." Intranets designed with specific newsrooms' needs in mind create a powerful portal to the Internet for journalists.

The major advantage of the intranet is the ability to gather the collective intelligence of the newsroom. The best, and most vital, intranets are those which allow the contribution by everyone in the newsroom of good resources found along the way. In newsrooms which provide "in-house sabbaticals" (time on the job where the journalist's task is to go "play on the Internet"), part of the payback for the "play-time" is the contribution of sites they found for the intranet and a "brown bag" lunch training session.

There is an excellent resource page about newsroom intranets on the Special Libraries Association – News Division Web site: *http://metalab. unc.edu/slanews/intranets/* Included there is some background on building an intranet as well as sample intranet pages.

Having an effective, up-to-date, well-organized and newsroom-tailored intranet may be one of the best ways to make use of the Internet effective and efficient for everyone in the newsroom.

Read More

"Fort Myers' 'Newsroom Intranet' Helps Provide Context, Depth": *http://www.gannett.com/go/newswatch/99/january/nw0108-1.htm*

Building Intranets: *http://www.ejc.nl/jr/intra/mainintranet.html* This resource page from the European Journalism Centre provides basics about the design and building of intranet pages.

COPYRIGHT ISSUES

I am no copyright expert but even I know that just because it's on the Web doesn't mean it's yours to use however you wish. Copyright is such a muddied area on the Web. The browser software makes it so easy to grab a photo, copy and paste some text, or download a file, but that doesn't mean you should.

In fact, many Web sites do provide their information with the intention that it be freely used and distributed. They say so on their Web page. But they do expect to have any material used to be attributed to them.

For example, this is the copyright policy on one site: "*Any item that appears in The Online Chronicle of Distance Education and Communication may be reproduced without permission. However, when this material is quoted or reproduced, the author and title of the item, as well as the issue of the Chronicle in which it appeared, must be cited.*"

Other Web sites, though, have, and intend to keep, copyright protection of their resources. "*The contents of The Boston School of Modern Languages, Inc. sites on the Internet are protected by applicable copyright laws. No permission is granted to copy, distribute, modify, post or frame any text, graphics, video, audio, software code, or user interface design or logos.*"

Copyright on the Web can be kind of murky. For example, Corbis, the huge picture site, has a huge collection of free downloads for people to send as greeting cards or as computer screen savers, but then there is an even larger collection of photos for which they want a payment if you intend to use it.

ArtToday, a huge clipart site: *http://www.arttoday.com* offers 40,000 free clipart images or 750,000 images if you pay $29.95 a year.

Many of my news research colleagues express their concerns about the apparent copyright infringement routinely going on in their newsrooms. It seems there needs to be some consciousness raising about what is, and isn't, free to use on the Web.

Here are some resources about copyright and the Web. I strongly suggest that if your newsroom does not have a policy about copyright that is clearly communicated to the folks in the newsroom that they do it soon.

Copyright resources

Selected Web sites on copyright and special libraries: *http://www. sla.org/membership/irc/copyrtweb.html* A nice bibliography of resources to use.

Guidelines on Creating Copyright Policies: *http://www.copyright.com/ News/Guidelines.html* From the Copyright Clearance Center.

Copyright Plain and Simple, by Cheryl Besenjak. Career Press, 1997.

Cyberspace Copyright: *http://www.poynter.org/research/hr/hr_052098. htm* One of Poynter researcher David Shedden's excellent bibliographies with many links to Web resources on the topic.

Hope Botterbusch's Copyright Site: *http://www.marine.usf.edu/ ~hopeb/* Focused on educators, but with helpful resources about building a copyright policy and useful links list.

MANAGING WEB SUBSCRIPTIONS

Jim Hunter, the research center director at the *Columbus Dispatch* e-mailed me about the situation with managing Internet accounts in their newsroom. *"The subscription sites on the Internet are a problem which continues to grow. Here are some examples:*

1. The commercial accounts are a headache – we are dealing with over 100 accounts on Nexis. My assistant director spends a fair amount of time adding, deleting, changing accounts and arranging training. The 100 accounts are about half what we need – we plan to retail Nexis accounts through the corporation/subsidiaries. We are also talking to Dow Jones which would work the same way.

2. Add to that, the AutoTrack problem – that is now Web-based and really should be in the hands of the people who need the service when we are not there. This could get expensive and we really have to worry about security/liability.

3. Additionally as we move to Version 4.0 of Preserver (AP's digital photo archive) which is Web-based and requires individual accounts there is another burden.

4. We are also moving to a Web-based text system (Vu/Text with a Web interface). I can see moving from generic logins to individual logins when we create better functionality.

5. Don't forget the numerous Web-based image sources (AP-Presslink and a lot of others that we require for sourcing images). We also have a due diligence issue with these accounts because we are dealing with copyrighted material, the misuse of which can hurt the paper. We have to keep careful track of who has those accounts and how they are using them."

Clearly, the issue is big and getting bigger as newsrooms move into end-user searching environments. Jim is talking about the mainstream commercial services and didn't even get into the Web subscriptions like E-Library or Northern Light or the *Wall Street Journal* Web site.

At Time Warner, News Research Center director Lany McDonald has managed Web subscriptions this way, "We have them divided by general subject – business, biography, news, reference – on a subscription intranet site we named InfoDesk. We have a charge-back situation, (*they charge the different magazines for library and research services*) so we've created an Access database of InfoDesk customer ID's and passwords. The Central Research Desk acts as the support staff for InfoDesk, and our trainer offers basic training as part of the monthly charges. Currently we have 12 subscription sites, plus some of our own information databases, but expect to grow this number this year."

There are no clear-cut solutions on how to deal with this but the important thing is to recognize early on that managing Web site subscriptions is going to be an issue that needs discussion or it will become unmanageable quickly.

Internet Use Policy Issues

Tom Pellegrene Jr., Manager of News Technologies at *The Journal Gazette* in Fort Wayne, Indiana, wrote about the Internet use policy at their newspaper:

"Basically, it says access to the Internet is company property much like notebooks and dictionaries are, so we are not to use our access for personal use...and we may not use the Internet to access sexually explicit material, even for an assignment, without the prior permission of the editor.

This actually came into play a few months ago, when a local resident was charged with practicing medicine without a license when he castrated people (who volunteered) in his home. We needed to understand why people might do that and allow it to be done to them, and we thought that in addition to calling experts, the Internet might be helpful. The editor granted permission to a reporter to look around castration-related sites, but the permission was limited to that person and that story."

In other newsrooms, the Internet use policy covers how e-mail can be used, how to attribute information found on the Web and other details of 'net usage.

A sample policy, written for the Associated Press, can be found at *http://PowerReporting/rules.html* This might give you some ideas of areas to cover in a policy. You might also talk with people on the online news staff about policy issues they might have (i.e., reporters answering e-mail from readers).

In conclusion

The move to the Internet-ed newsroom is going to create some situations which, if not anticipated, will short circuit all the best attempts at getting this resource available to the journalists and researchers who need it. Getting the newsroom wired is only the first step. The next steps will involve training, understanding and managing this vast information resource.

Keeping Up On the Internet

Tips and Techniques on how to stay up with the latest and best Web sites and Internet techniques....

This guide has just been a kick start for using the Internet. There will be constant updates to Web sites and new techniques for research coming out all the time. Great new resources will be made available that you'll want to know about. How can you keep up with it all?

There are a number of techniques you can use to stay up-to-date with the Internet and Web resources.

Subscribe to Discussion Lists

- CARR-L: Computer-Assisted Reporting and Research
    subscribe address: *listserv@ulkyvm.louisville.edu*
- Newslib: News Librarians Listserv
    subscribe address: *listserv@gibbs.oit.unc.edu*
- IRE-L: Investigative Reporters and Editors
    subscribe address: *listproc@lists.missouri.edu*
- NICAR-L: National Institute for Computer Assisted Reporting
    subscribe address: *listproc@lists.missouri.edu*
- SPJ: Society for Professional Journalists
    subscribe address: *listserv@psuvm.psu.edu*
- Government Resources: subscribe address: *lwarren@well.com*
- Find Beat Specific listservs at Topica: *http://www.topica.com*

Stay up with changes in specific sites with e-mail alerts

- Use NetMind: *http://mindit.netmind.com* or Informant: *http://informant.dartmouth.edu*

Read magazines

- **Yahoo!: Internet Life:** *http://www.zdnet.com/yil/*
- **Online:** *http://www.onlineinc.com/onlinemag/index.html*
- **Database:** *http://www.onlineinc.com/database/index.html*: past articles
- **EContent:** *http://www.ecmag.com* – formerly Database magazine
- **Searcher:** *http://www.infotoday.com/searcher/default.htm*
- **Cyber-Skeptic's Digest:** *http://www.bibliodata.com/skeptic/skepdata.html*
- **Internet Newsroom:** *http://www.editors-service.com/*
- **Uplink/Nicar:** *http://www.nicar.org*
- **IRE Journal:** *http://www.ire.org*

Monitor WHAT'S NEW sites

- Yahoo!: *http://www.yahoo.com*
- "What's new" on specific sites

Subscribe to the SCOUT REPORT

- Science & Engineering, Social Sciences, Business & Economics: *http://scout.cs.wisc.edu/scout/report/*

Reporting Tasks/Internet Tools

The main focus of this guide has been how to clearly define your reporting task. In this section, I point to a few specific tools you can to which will help with specific tasks.

FIND EXPERTS

Look for academic or think tank experts

- Send a message to ProfNet: *http://www.profnet.com/reporters.html* with a description of what kind of expertise you need
- Look for a professor in the ProfNet database: *http://www.profnet. com/ped.html*
- Check out the Experts Resource List: U.S. and Int'l Sources with links to dozens of expert directories. Compiled by *St. Petersburg Times* researcher Kitty Bennett: *http://metalab.unc.edu/slanews/ internet/experts.html*
- The **National Press Club** library has an experts database: *http://npc.press.org/sources*

Look for the author of a book on the topic

- Look in **Amazon:** *http://www.amazon.com* for authors. To locate them, connect to their publisher's site and get a contact name to call to ask how to get in touch with them
- Check out authors in the **Library of Congress: Subject Search** form: *http://lcWeb.loc.gov/catalog/browse/bks3subj.html*

Look for a government official to talk with

- **WhoWhere: U.S. Government:** *http://www.whowhere.com/ Govt/main.html*
- **Federal Telephone Directories:** *http://www.info.gov/fed_ directory/phone.htm*
- **Governments Online:** EU and other European govt. links, most have personnel directories: *http://europa.eu.int/gonline_en.html*
- **European Political Resources:** a links page to country governments, parties and associations: *http://www.agora.stm.it/politic/ europe.htm*
- **Chiefs of State and Cabinet Members:** *http://www.odci.gov/cia/ publications/chiefs*

Find someone in a business that deals with the topic

- **GTE SuperPages:** *http://yp.superpages.com* Enter a type of business and pick your state (Doing a story about asbestos in the schools and need to find asbestos removal companies – type asbestos in the category...)

Find a magazine or newsletter on the topic – contact the editors and ask them for writers on the topic

- **MediaFinder:** *http://www.oxbridge.com/custom.cfm*
- **PubList:** *http://www.publist.com*

Check a Web site which locates subject experts

- **Pitsco's Ask an Expert:** *http://www.askanexpert.com/*

FIND PEOPLE WITH EXPERIENCE

- Search messages from people who have had that experience in **Deja's** archive of newsgroup messages: *http://www.deja.com*

- **eGroups:** archive of eGroups sponsored listserv messages *http://www.findmail.com*

- Find people with different medical conditions in the **Mediconsult** support groups: *http://www.mediconsult.com/*

- Contact an association and see if they can connect you with someone with experience. Find one at the **Virtual Community of Associations:** *http://www.vcanet.org/vca/assns.htm* or check out **Associations Unlimited** – the e-version of Encyclopedia of Associations (there is a subscription fee): *http://www.gale.com/gale/galenet/galenet.html*

- Check out personal Web pages on Web rings, find them at **WebRing**: *http://www.webring.org*

GET BACKGROUND INFORMATION

On famous people: past and present

- **Biography.com:** over 20,000 bios on current and past personalities: *http://www.biography.com*

- **Biographical Dictionary:** over 25,000 bios: *http://www.s9.com/biography/*

- **Information Please Almanac:** click on the "People" section: *http://www.infoplease.com/*

On Congressmen

- **Biographical Directory of the United States Congress, 1774 to Present:** *http://bioguide.congress.gov/*

On foreign affairs and political issues

- **ForeignWire:** *http://www.foreignwire.com* Packages of information on selected issues and events

- **House of Commons Library Research Papers:** *http://www.parliament.uk/commons/lib/research/rpintro.htm* Written for Members of Parliament by the staff of the library – research on everything from Bovine Tuberculosis to NATO's New Direction to the Crime and Disorder bill

- **Congressional Research Reports:** *http://gwis2.circ.gwu.edu/~gprice/crs.htm*

On toxic chemicals

- **Toxic Release Inventory:** *http://www.epa.gov/enviro/html/tris/tris_query_java.html* from the Environmental Protection Agency

On a date

- **Daily Globe:** *http://www.dailyglobe.com/day2day.html* Searchable date archive with esoteric events and anniversaries

On a nonprofit or charity
- **Guidestar:** *http://www.guidestar.org/* Financial information on more than 600,000 charities

On a company
- **Hoovers:** *http://www.hoovers.com* "The ultimate source for company information."
- **PR Newswire:** *http://www.prnewswire.com* Press Releases.

On a drug
- **Mayo Clinic MedicineCenter: USP Drug Guide** *http://www.mayohealth.org/usp/common/index.htm*

On a disease
- **Center for Disease Control:** *http://www.cdc.gov/search.htm*
- **Mediconsult.com:** *http://www.mediconsult.com* Look up a disease and find all kinds of supporting information
- **Healthfinder:** *http://www.healthfinder.gov* Find associations and fact sheets from the government about different diseases

FIND FACTS AND STATISTICS

About a country
- **CIA World Factbook:** *http://www.odci.gov/cia/publications/factbook/index.html*
- **Country Studies from the U.S. Library of Congress:** *http://lcweb2.loc.gov/frd/cs/cshome.html*

Make calculations, do conversions
- **Calculators On-Line Center:** *http://www-sci.lib.uci.edu/HSG/RefCalculators.html* 100s of topics
- **Currency converter:** *http://www.oanda.com/converter/classic*
- **MapQuest:** *http://www.mapquest.com*
- **Find distance between zip codes:** *http://link-usa.com/zipcode/*
- **Find distance between cities:** *http://www.indo.com/distance/*

Locate statistics sources
- **FedStats:** *http://www.fedstats.gov*
- **Statistical Resources on the Web:** *http://www.lib.umich.edu/libhome/Documents.center/stats.html* Organized by topic, links to sites with statistics
- **Statistical Sites on the World Wide Web:** *http://www.bls.gov/oreother.htm* Links to the main statistics sites for different countries

Locate crime statistics
- **Sourcebook of Criminal Justice Statistics:** *http://www.albany.edu/sourcebook*

Find ready reference information (gazetteers, dictionaries, almanacs)
- **Internet Public Library:** *http://www.ipl.org/ref/RR* Organized by type of reference – almanac, dictionary…
- **Web of Online Dictionaries:** *http://www.facstaff.bucknell.edu/rbeard/diction.html* More than 500 dictionaries in 140 different languages.

- **Infomine: Scholarly Internet Resources:** *http://infomine.ucr.edu/reference*
- **Information Please Almanac:** *http://www.infoplease.com/*

Get "Top…." and ranking lists
- **Price's List of Lists:** *http://gwis2.circ.gwu.edu/~gprice/listof.htm*

Find polls and survey results
- **Pew Center:** *http://www.people-press.org/*
- **Gallup:** *http://www.gallup.com/*

FIND SOURCE DOCUMENTS

Locate laws and constitutions of different countries
- **U.S. House of Representatives – Laws of other nations:** *http://law.house.gov/52.htm* Plus other key documents/speeches
- **Guide to Law Online – Nations of the World:** *http://lcweb2.loc.gov/glin/x-nation.html*

Locate U.S. Government documents, speeches
- President's Speeches/Statements: *http://www.whitehouse.gov*
- Legislative Information: Thomas: *http://thomas.loc.gov*
- Govbot: Database of Government Web sites: *http://ciir2.cs.umass.edu/Govbot/*

Find historical documents from the U.S.
- **American Memory Project** from the Library of Congress: *http://memory.loc.gov*

Get Supreme Court decisions
- **Findlaw:** *http://www.findlaw.com/casecode/supreme.html*

Get company reports
- **Annual Report Gallery: U.S. companies:** *http://www.report-gallery.com*
- <Search tip: find company documents on their Web sites…try www.companyname.com (for U.S.) or www.companyname.co.uk>

Find documents in United Nations Organizations Websites
- **UNIONS:** United Nations International Organizations Network Search: *http://www3.itu.int/unions/*

Find a quotation
- **Quote Search:** *http://www.starlingtech.com/quotes/search.html*

KEEP UP ON YOUR BEAT

- Get **story ideas**, tap into what people are talking about in the area of your beat:
- Monitor specific newsgroups: **Deja:** *http://www.deja.com*
- Subscribe to a listserv or two on the topic you cover routinely – find them at **Topica:** *http://www.topica.com*
- Locate a few **key Web sites** for your beat and read the "what's new" area:
  - Locate federal government Web sites at: http://www.lib.lsu.edu/gov/fedgov.html

- Locate state and local government Web sites at: *http://www.piperinfo.com/state/states.html*

■ Keep up with the key **magazines** in your area by checking the online edition: Find the magazines and see if they are on the Web with Publist: *http://www.publist.com*

SOME GREAT JOURNALISTS' SITES FOR JOURNALISTS

Instead of providing yet another subject-based bookmark list (which, in book form, would be dreadfully out of date soon), I thought that pointing out places, and people, on the Web who are maintaining great listings of resources for journalists would be better. Take a look at these sites, bookmark a few you think would be particularly useful to you, and send an e-mail of appreciation to the folks who put them together and maintain them for you!

- **A Journalist's Database of Databases**

http://www.reporter.org/~drew/database.html

Drew Sullivan's awesome collection of searchable databases on the Internet, for tracking leads, finding ideas, providing context.

- **Barbara's News Researcher's Page:** *http://www.gate.net/~barbara/index.html*

Palm Beach Post researcher Barbara Shapiro has maintained this list of subject-organized links for years now. She also started the Journalism and Research Web ring (Hacks).

- **European Journalism Centre's Journalists' Toolbox:** *http://www.ejc.nl/jr/toolbox.html*

Particularly good resources for the coverage of European Union issues as well as general guides to journalist resources.

- **Facsnet:** *http://www.facsnet.org*

Former journalist and journalism professor Randy Reddick is the master of this Web of valuable Internet Resources (organized by broad and then narrower topics within the broad topic). The entries in the resource guide have great annotations explaining what of value journalists will find in the site. Check out, too, the Top Issues, Reporting Tools and Sources Online sections.

- **Journalism Net:** *http://www.journalismnet.com/*

Canadian journalist and trainer Julian Sher's homepage of resources of journalists. Well organized by type of resource with special sections for UK, U.S., Canadian, and French journalists. Check out his story topics section for great sites to track down good ideas.

- **Librarians' Links:** *http://www.microserve.net:80/~library/*

A great example of a "newsroom organized" resource page by the library staff at the *Patriot-News*, in Harrisburg, PA. Organized by beats: Business, Courts, Crime, Environment, etc., and Features: Art, Biography, Books, Consumers, Diversity, etc., the listing is annotated and well-selected.

- **Megasources:** *http://www.ryerson.ca/journal/megasources.html*

Dean Tudor, Professor at the School of Journalism at Ryerson Polytechnic University in Toronto, has an extensive subject-based list of bookmarks. No annotations to the entries, but the site is regularly updated with the best new finds.

- **New York Times CyberTimes Navigator:** *http://www.nytimes.com/navigator*

Rich Meislin's listing of resources has a special list of links to collections of interest to journalists.

- **PC Mike** *http://www.pcmike.com/*

Broadcast journalist and author of *Wired Journalist* Mike Wendland's, site contains excellent tipsheets and "what's happening" newsletter about all manner of computing and Internet use.

- **Power Reporting** *http://PowerReporting.com*

Bill Dedman's links to bookmarks and some tutorials on Web searching.

- **Poynter Institute: Yesterday's Headlines:** *http://www.poynter.org/research/reshotres.htm*

Valuable Web resources on current and precious news topics compiled by Poynter researcher David Shedden. Also, find the bookmark lists to sites in this guide at *http://www.poynter.org/research/newcar*

- **Price's Lists** *http://gwis2.circ.gwu.edu/~gprice/direct.htm*

Gary Price's compilations of incredibly useful, and often hidden, resources on the 'Net: Direct Search (a listing of databases by topic), Speech/Transcript Center, Audio and Video on the Web (links to audio and video sites worldwide), List of Lists (top 10, top 100…)

- **Reporter.org** *http://www.reporter.org*

The homepage for the IRE/NICAR journalism sites mall. Links to lots of organizations, each with great resources on CAR and aids for journalists using the net.

- **Reporter's Desktop** *http://www.reporter.org/desktop*

Duff Wilson's compilation of key reference/research tools for journalists with the search boxes provided. Finding people, background and Web searches.

- **Schlein's Deadline Online:** *http://www.deadlineonline.com*

Alan Schlein's compilation, with explanation, of key resources for journalists.

- **Special Libraries Association/News Division**
http://metalab.unc.edu/slanews/

The homepage for the News Division of SLA where you'll find helpful guides to various resources: newspaper archives on the Web, expert directories on the Web (organized geographically and by topic), examples of newsroom Intranet sites.

INDEX

Links To Web Sites: By Chapter

CHAPTER 1: 3-20

- We're all nerds now, by Joel Simon and Carol Napolitano. Columbia Journalism Review, March / April 1999. *http://www.cjr.org/year/99/2/nerds.asp*

- Bibliography on Computer Assisted Reporting. Poynter Institute. *http://www.poynter.org/research/biblio/bib_car.htm*

- Handouts and articles on CAR. Poynter Institute: *http://www.poynter.org/research/car.htm*

- IRE Resource Center: *http://www.ire/org/resourcecenter/*

CHAPTER 2: 21-58

A conceptual view of the Internet: 23-24

- Media in Cyberspace poll: *http://www.middleberg.com/sub_cyberspace study.html*

- The Usually Useful Internet Guide for Journalists: *http://www.usus.org/*

- Understanding and using the Internet: *http://www.pbs.org/uti/*

E-Mail: 24-31

Tracking E-mail Virus Hoaxes

- Urban Legends: Computer Virus Hoaxes: *http://urbanlegends.about.com*
- Computer Virus Myths: *http://kumite.com/myths/*

E-mail policy sample:

- Associated Press: *http://PowerReporting.com/rules.html*

General E-Mail Directories: (primarily US e-mail)

- WhoWhere: *http://www.whowhere.com.*
- Internet Address Finder: *http://www.iaf.net*
- Yahoo! People Search: *http://people.yahoo.com*
- InfoSpace: *http://www.infospace.com.*
- MESA: MetaEmailSearchAgent: *http://mesa.rrzn.uni-hannover.de/*
- Usenet Addresses: *http://usenet-addresses.mit.edu*
- PeopleSearch: *http://peoplesearch.net*

International E-Mail Directories:

- World E-Mail Directory: *http://www.worldemail.com/wede4e.shtml*
- Infobel: *http://www.infobel.be/internet/email.asp*

Specialty E-Mail Directories:

- Congressional E-Mail Directory at *http://www.webslingerz.com/jhoffman/congress-email.html*

Free e-mail services

- Yahoo!: *http://mail.yahoo.com*
- My Own Email: *http://www.myownemail.com*
- RocketMail: *http://www.rocketmail.com*